MW00876630

Quotes from Amazon readers from the first edition.

Mary B. said, "Matthew Gewinner is a troubled young man. He has, however, worked his way back from the brink of destruction and then shares his story to help others dealing with similar issues."

Miranda Reads said, "Matthew provides a very real look into what is like to live with mental illness and his struggles to overcome his addictions."

John G. Said, "My wife calls the book a 'page-turner' and it details how a life can really spiral downward, in darkness and without hope. We see him then take the first steps to the other side of life, the good side."

Angie said, "This book is = to confessing sins. Congratulations to putting yourself on display which takes a hugeeeee amount of effort and self conviction. This is a fantastic very 1st person view on real life and dealing with the judgements and labels that come with it. Worded from raw conviction."

Lee F. said, "This book helped me realize the effects it has. Interesting read on how BPD affected this individual."

Inside the mind of a Borderline Personality, My Life & Recovery from BPD 2nd Edition

By Matthew J. Gewinner

Contact Info:
Email: borderlines2018@gmail.com
Phone #314-810-6692

The people in this book have been given alternate names, in order to protect their identities.

Table of Contents

Preface

I want to begin to warn you that this is not a book that glorifies BPD behaviors or symptoms. This book is about a child who becomes a man who has lived various parts of his life undiagnosed and diagnosed.

Even though I was officially diagnosed with BPD in my late twenties. This book takes you through my life as an undiagnosed who is very symptomatic as a child. Then diagnosed for the first time as a teen, who is very symptomatic and on and offs meds. Next, it will take you to the point I am off medications with symptoms that are hidden by my lifestyle. While following up in my twenties off meds and self-medicating while symptomatic. Lastly, toward the end of the book, I get an official diagnosis.

The book is designed to show the reader how living with mental health symptoms in the present can affects one's life greatly. As you will read. Since I've experienced symptoms in full force on a daily basis it made my daily living to even monthly living extremely difficult as you will see through the problems I faced and the choices that I made.

That diagnoses will be BPD, Bipolar, and Narcissistic and OCD traits, which might be an OCPD diagnosis. This is around the time when I am thirty which I then go into long-term therapy and focus on getting better and healthy. For the first time, I'm fully committed to treatment, with hopes of a better way of life.

This book's goal is to show the reader what it is like to live with mental health symptoms in full force. The book also shows the reader how mental health symptoms can affect one's life.

Chapter 1: Introduction

I am Matthew, and this is my story. I was established on August 5th, 1982, and I have struggled with some mental health conditions, which are: Borderline Personality Disorder, Bipolar I, and Narcissistic and OCD traits. I am an alcoholic and my sobriety date is August 8th, 2013. I was born and raised in St. Louis, Missouri, which seems like a town I could never get away from no matter how much I ran from it.

I'm writing my story so that I can help others out there who are struggling with similar issues as I have had in my past. I've read many books and memoirs on alcoholism and mental illnesses, which I have found very helpful when dealing with my own conditions knowing I'm not alone out there in this cold dark world that I live in. I've experienced loss and in my grief, became disconnected from the world that surrounds me. During that time, I've battled drug and alcohol addiction along with having untreated mental health conditions. Moreover, I've self-medicated during my mid to late teens and into my late twenties, before I fell into treatment seeking the help I needed, because I couldn't do it alone. Even though I have been in and out of treatment before and hospitalized for my psychiatric illnesses to get the help I needed; I wasn't ready for it at that time, unfortunately, no matter how hard anybody tried to help me I wouldn't comply or conform. I was pissed off at the world, and I would let it know through my actions and behaviors. Nobody could stop me from my self-destructive behaviors. I was on a hell-bound train with a one-way ticket to hell. There was no coming back or so I thought.

I've self-medicated to numb myself from feeling anything, which caused more problems in my life then one would welcome. In addition, I'm what people would call a "cutter." During my dark times, I would cut to know that I could still feel and that I was alive and not dead on the outside because I felt dead on the inside down to my very soul.

I've experienced a black world of loneliness due to my subconscious desire to push people away, such as if I was wearing a big black sign saying, "Not Welcome!" During my times of dark despair while ingesting mass amounts of alcohol I'd drink till the point of having blackouts. If you would ask me back then, what I thought of having a blackout? I would have said, "It's fun not knowing what you did the night before because then I could peace back together the night of the blackout." During all my turmoil, I have lost many close friends, such as Katy, Jeremy, Eric, Brandon, Mo, and Chrissy. Not to mention the handful of caring friends I pushed away, which I will get into in a later chapter.

Again, leaving me lost and all alone in this cold dark world. They may be gone, but they are not forgotten, not one bit. To this very day, I still think of them daily, and they will always hold a spot in my heart. I've lost these friends due to freak accidents, such as suicide, drug overdoses, and murder. I visit Katy's, Jeremy's, and Chrissy's grave on their anniversaries. I'm leaving out family that I've lost because I don't consider myself close to any member of the Gewinner family. Those would include a cousin that died at birth, two Grandfathers, but I hold the Grandfather on my father's side more highly due to all his incredible accomplishments. In addition to two Grandmothers, but one died before I was born, and she too came from my father's side of the family, which left me with a Step-Grandmother. With so much loss you might see why I've pushed people away if I think that they will abandon me and die. Why bother trying anymore, right?

While coping with the deaths of my friends for a few years I overindulged in drug and alcohol abuse. During this time, I was blind to how my current choices were screwing up my chances at college and having a hockey career while in college. By eighteen years of age, I decided to drop out of high school with my GED and join the U.S. Army to become a combat medic. I found the other men in the Army was a family I have been looking for since my drug friends were not a trustworthy family. Even though I was a full-blown alcohol and drug addict before I joined the military, and here is where I would say my alcohol addiction took off like a rocket heading to outer space. Deep outer space that is. I was in the military for just under four years. Moreover, I even managed to marry too, but that lasted three months and was one of my main reasons I decided to leave the Army and head home, back to the dreaded town of St. Louis.

I'm officially discharged from the Army and now a veteran. Once I got back to St. Louis I never bothered to use my VA benefits for mental health reasons, because of all the horror stories I had heard about the VA system being crappy. Not to mention the fact that I was still drinking with the use of increasing amounts of alcohol daily, and I was still self-medicating with any drug that crossed my path. Flash forward about eight or nine years, and I am using the VA to receive psychiatric medications, but the whole VA system and their psychologist or psychiatrist are still useless in my opinion. On the bright side, I am able to receive medication that I need to help manage my symptoms.

I turned twenty-one right before I left the Army and in the months leading up to my departure, one could tell I was an alcoholic by all standards. Since I crashed my car before my departure date so I ended up taking a bus across the country back home to St. Louis. The town that keeps pulling me back. I'm twenty-one now and looking for a job with my skills that I've learned as a combat medic.

Who would have thought there would be so many companies, hospitals, and doctors' offices that would refuse people with military training, hence my first job search was difficult. Eventually, I found a job with a doctor, which practiced Internal Medicine. I stayed with that same doctor for eight years. Then it was time for me to pre-sue other career options, and I went back to college. Mind you I am still drinking mass amounts of alcohol daily to escape my horrid pain.

At first, it was not my decision to go back to college, but I did have some help from my clinical psychologist Dr. Bemer on encouraging me that I could afford it and that I would do well in college. I hadn't seen Dr. Bemer for long, about a handful of months, but she had gained my trust quickly. She was probably one of the only people that I've trusted at that time in my life. I haven't seen Dr. Bemer for years now, but I still think of her from time to time and how she has helped me greatly, but since our departure I've had a handful of other doctors, psychologists, therapists, and consulars that I've seen, but I haven't been happy with most of them. Hence they don't have my complete trust, which means I manipulate them as I see fit while playing head games with them for my personal pleasure.

I enrolled in St. Louis Community College, and I was there for two semesters. When I left to seek more in-depth treatment I was officially a sophomore in college; my GPA was 3.8, but it would have been a 4.0 if I didn't have the trouble I did during the last semester of finals (mental health-wise). I was still invited to become a member of Phi Theta Kappa, which is an academic honor society. The degrees I am pursuing are Bachelors in Psychology, Masters in Sociology, and finally a Ph.D. in Abnormal Psychology with a focus on Neuro-Psychology. Since I have only completed one year of undergrad I will have a long way to go, but I now leave that up to my higher power on where my academic pursuits take me.

My choice to seek treatment with Dr. Bemer was on my own because I knew I was in bad shape and needed help. Having had weekly blackouts and waking up in a crimson sea of blood. She asked that I cut back on the drinking while I was in college, but that I couldn't do. I lied to her when she asked me if I had cut back at our appointments. She expressed her desire to have me put on medication, but I had to stop drinking first. That was something I couldn't do at that time. The booze had a hold on me like the Devil's grip. I made it through my first two semesters of college and one class in summer school, but then my world came crashing down on me, and my life seemed like a total loss. The next phase of my treatment would be in Lexington, Kentucky for around 14 months.

At this point in my life, I really wanted the treatment, but it still had its ups and downs, especially as I was being put on and off medication trying to find something that would work for my conditions. In those 14 months, I was very symptomatic, which made things difficult for everybody around me, such as fellow treatment mates, clinician, staff, and doctors.

After treatment in Lexington, I came back to St. Louis but was being treated in Farmington Missouri. I went for individual sessions once a week for a handful of months that eventually turned into two years. In the beginning, I went through three different therapists before I found one I felt safe talking with. Her name was Maria. I've continued to see her for many months after our initial visit. We have been able to get a lot of work done in improving my mental health symptoms and coping with them in my life.

Currently, I am out of intensive treatment and I see Maria twice a month for two hours per session. I attend AA meetings regularly, about 3-4 a week. Sometimes more. I have noticed changes in myself, thought patterns, not having a need to drink, and even a dramatic lowering of cutting "episodes." Having said that I still have had mental health symptoms from time to time, but I do my best to cope with the ways I know how to that are healthy for me.

Chapter 2: Alcoholism and Mental Health Criteria

Before I begin my story, I will take the time to go through the mental health criteria one would have to meet to have my diagnoses. I am duel diagnosed, meaning I have a substance abuse disorder, in addition, to a few mental health conditions.

The DSM IV (TR) states that people must meet a certain number of criteria to be diagnosed with a condition, such as for Borderline Personality Disorder (which is one of my diagnoses) one would have to meet five or more of the nine criteria specified. First, let's look at alcohol addiction before I get into the numerous mental health conditions that I am diagnosed with.

According to Alcoholics Anonymous, anybody can deem them-self an alcoholic. Furthermore, they have pamphlets that ask questions, and one's answers determine a number that will show you if you should consider yourself an alcoholic or not, but they are only suggestions whether to seek treatment or help in Alcoholics Anonymous. Some of those questions would be: Do you drink more than two drinks a day? Do you drink more than you intended to on any given occasion? Have you ever blacked out from drinking? Does alcohol inter-fear with your everyday lifestyle? , and so forth. I think you get the idea. I always scored very high on these questionnaires, but I never cared as I didn't believe the suggestions they have to offer.

Hi, my name is Matt, and I am an alcoholic. I started drinking in high school or thereabouts, which was normal everyday teenage behavior, at least in my town. I did drink alcohol as a child, but I never got drunk like in high school. But then it took a turn for the worse when my two close friends died back to back. Their names were Jeremy and Katy. I was angry and mad at this so-called God person who took them from me prematurely. I'm sixteen at the time.

Katy and Jeremy's deaths affected me greatly. I couldn't understand while I was a Christian at this time, why would God take the closest people from me. I was deeply saddened and as my drug and alcohol use took off; I lost my faith, eventually becoming an Atheists. God and screwed me so in retaliation I denied his existence altogether.

My weekend drinking picked up in the amounts of booze I was pouring down my throat. I spent all my free time trying to get alcohol, and I was drinking during the day when I had nothing going on and while at school too. When it was difficult to obtain alcohol, I sought out many different types of street drugs as well. I mainly consumed marijuana during the days and nights, in addition, to drinking booze. The drugs that I have used in my past have been: marijuana, ecstasy, cocaine, LSD, mushrooms, CO_2 cans (wip-its), and a variety of colorful pills.

The first step of AA says, "We admitted we were powerless over alcohol -- that our lives became unmanageable." I didn't believe this until I figured out what true powerlessness meant to me. I was 30/31 at the time when I figured it out. But I was in AA much sooner than that around age 17/18. I was very hostile in my early meetings believing that I did not have a problem with drugs or alcohol. Plus, not to mention the fact I didn't know why I was even there. I regret not being open-minded at 17/18 years of age because since then I have lost my entire twenties due to my alcohol and drug addiction.

What is an addiction? It's different for different people, but I will explain my definition here. Powerlessness. What does that mean? As I figured this out by the end of my twenties I had become dumbfounded with myself and deeply sadden due to the years I lost. An example of powerlessness over alcohol would be of me driving to the liquor store on my way home from work at 5 pm to buy booze in the middle of a gigantic snow storm.

I remember picking up my favorite beer and whiskey standing in line, and as I looked around I saw everybody buying bread and milk, shit like that to make it through the storm. One man even commented to me that I was getting the essentials. He was correct at that time in my life, moreover, what he didn't know was that if I had finished all my booze by the middle of the night that I would be headed back out in my car and face the snowstorm to obtain more liquor, while being heavily intoxicated and not caring what could have happened to me. I was a hazard to myself. Keep in mind on that night I was buying a bottle of Jack Daniels and two twelve packs of Milwaukie Best, but I was still concerned with running out of liquor. Powerlessness is when you try to start drinking at 10 am and as you pour the booze down your gullet your own body rejects the alcohol causing you to vomit instantly. That didn't even matter for me, because I kept forcing the alcohol down my throat until it stayed down, and I could continue to drink in peace after the violent vomiting, numbing myself from the reality that I lived in this so-called life. This is just a glimpse of my alcoholism to come.

I realized I had an alcohol problem at this point but the addiction was so strong that it compelled me to continue pouring booze down my throat, no matter what.

I have been diagnosed with a handful of mental health conditions all by a doctor or psychologist, none are self-diagnosed. My current diagnoses are borderline personality disorder, bipolar I, depression at one time in my life, OCD and Narcissist traits. For one to have met the criteria for a full diagnosis, one would have to have meet x number of criteria out of y number of criteria available. What are the traits then? Traits are when you meet some of the criteria listed, but not enough for a full diagnosis.

The criteria for borderline personality disorder is one who has, "A pervasive pattern of instability of interpersonal relationships, self-image and affects, and marked impulsivity beginning by early adulthood and present in a variety of contexts, as indicated by five (or more) of the following:

1.) Frantic efforts to avoid real or imagined abandonment. Note: Do not include suicidal or self-mutilating behavior covered in criteria 5. (this is one criteria I meet)

2.) A pattern of unstable and intense interpersonal relationships characterized by alternating between extremes of idealization and devaluation. (I meet this one too)

3.) Identity disturbance: markedly and persistently unstable self-image or sense of self. (and this one as well that I meet.)

4.) Impulsivity in at least two areas that are potentially self-damaging (e.g. spending, sex, substance abuse, reckless driving, binge eating). Note: Do not include suicidal or self-mutilating behavior covered in Criterion 5.

5.) Recurrent suicidal behavior, gestures, threats, or self-mutilating behavior. (I'm covered in meeting 4 & 5 here too.)

6.) Affective instability due to a marked reactivity of mood (e.g. intense episodic dysphoria, irritability, or anxiety usually lasting a few hours and only rarely more than a few days. (I fall into this criteria too)

7.) Chronic feelings of emptiness. (Yes, this one too.) Some doctors will add chronic boredom here, but that varies on the doctor you are speaking with.

8.) Inappropriate, intense anger or difficulty controlling anger (e.g. frequent displays of temper, constant anger, recurrent physical fights.) (I'm in this one also.)

9.) Transient, stress-related paranoid ideation or severe dissociative symptoms. (This one could be up for debate for me.)

As you can see that I meet eight out of the nine criteria for Borderline Personality disorder. I realized that me just telling you this is not much of a convincer so I will now go through the criteria and examples of how I meet them.

Criteria one talks about using chaotic efforts to avoid abandonment real or imagined. When I lost my friends in high school I became suspicious of any new potential friends, but at the same time, I could be overly clingy to people I just met. There is a book called, "I Hate You, Don't Leave Me". That pretty much sums up my actions towards people that I allowed in my life. One minute I am holding onto them with dear life, and the next I am kicking those people out the window. Only to call them back hours or days later. As one might see being around a person like this could be quite confusing due to their nonconforming behavior.

I had a female friend (an old co-worker) named Britney. Once I left the company we both worked for I friended her on Facebook. We began hanging out and fooling around. During those times, I was in a drunken stupor, or well I was just drunk all the time. I would verbally unload on her if she made a mistake in my texting rules that she was unaware of, or I'd kick her out of my apartment moments after we had finished fooling around. I'd call her and yell at her that I wanted her to never talk to me again, or then I'd send her messages asking why she never called anymore. After about two months of this, she finally went out and got another boyfriend since I was so confused about our relationship together. When I heard this, I was hurt and very confused as to her actions as I thought we still had something going on. Then were my attempts to get her back or demanded she treat my calls as they were in the first few weeks when we were fooling around, and then when Britney became angry with me I demanded attention, or I would never speak to her again for eternity.

This is only one example as there have been many other times I went through this with people some didn't even know I was in distress about losing them while others received the brunt of my verbal attacks. This falls right into criteria number two.

The second criteria speaks about one showing a pattern of unstable and intense relationships dramatized by extreme idealization and devaluation. Many of my relationships fall here. You might notice that with the Britney story. One minute I hate them (devaluation) the next I think the world of them (idealization). Again, pointing out the book title, "I Hate You, Don't Leave Me." Just in case you didn't know that book was written to explain the borderline behaviors to help others understand who we are in a sense as a person.

A lot of people that have encountered me have no clue the many times over I have either idealized them or devalued them to pound scum or worse in my mind. For me, it is very black and white thinking when it comes to other people's actions. This is another hallmark of borderlines. It's all or nothing type of thinking, black and white. Then I see them as having slighted me, or I hold them up on

36

high, which would make me think they are just the greatest person in the world. What's the worst part for myself and these people not knowing is when I felt hurt by their actions it often led to self-harm or "cutting" episodes upon myself. Feeling hurt is like when you see a little boy with one flower running to give it to his dream girl, and as he rounds the corner he sees another boy already talking with her. Then he just turns and walks away, head down and completely crushed as the flower begins to wilt and die as he walks away.

     I still idealize people from time to time and devalue them in the same note. But I try to tell myself it's not me to judge them. So, I have built a wall around myself vowing that nobody will ever get in. This wall compares to the great wall of China that is around me, and as my therapist points out that there are no windows for people to look in and say, "Hello", while making efforts to be my friend. Currently, I'm trying to build some windows on my wall, but the outlook is grim as I don't want to experience the risk of rejection or loss again. My wall defends me when I can't defend myself. It's a protectant from me and the outside world.

The next criteria are about identity disturbance of ones-self. Since I was born I never felt comfortable in my own skin. Kind of like the feeling of wearing someone's else's shoes or something of the sorts maybe even someone's underwear. That is how uncomfortable I felt in my own skin. I never felt like I belonged in any one group of people so I tried many of them out. By seven I was a hockey player and damn good one by age ten. I've worn the hat of a magician for a couple of years. I was a combat medic, street racer, medical assistant, drug dealer/addict, college student, mental patient, intellectual, rock star, the reader, but in many of those, I felt that I truly didn't belong, or that I was an imposter, and they would find it out eventually. Somehow I decided to come up with my own identity as a combination of things, but there is this feeling like something missing. Without that something whatever it may be I feel as there is a hollow piece inside of me and without that, I may never be whole.

What is impulsivity? The fourth criteria states for someone who is impulsive in two or more areas that are potentially self-damaging. Some of those areas to name a few are spending, sex, substance abuse, reckless driving, and binge eating. I have some of these on my list, but depending on who I am at the time I tend to interchange them like people swapping DVDs at a Redbox location. Cutting and self-harm do not fall into this category as well as with suicidal gestures and behaviors. These areas will be coved in criteria five.

I have driven recklessly while I used my car in street racing. Not to mention just driving recklessly as to include speeding, running stop signs, lights, etc. I generally drove my car as fast as I could not really caring what the outcome was with complete disregard for my life and others as well. Having the car go fast and faster as the speedometer climbed up was a rush no one can explain until they've experienced it. It was a true feeling of freedom from all the bondage that holds me down.

My second area would be sex. Keep in mind that these areas flip-flop from time to time depending on my current identity. Throughout my life, I have lived on a sexual edge. I've had numerous partners, some on a one on one basis and others in more of a group type situation. My sex behavior has been completely reckless, such as I hardly ever wore condoms. Luckily enough I have had no STDs or kids that I am aware of to show for it. I've even tested myself fully after two-plus years of abstinence during my early sobriety. Despite my longing for a real relationship I've been more the one-night stand type of guy in my past. There have been repeating performances though. It's not that I ever mistreated a female, but I consider sex with one another as the most intimate way to get to know that person, and once that has happened there is no more you can know about that person in a sense, or on a physical level. Thus, the reason for abandoning them before they can abandon me. You may see some of these behaviors in my younger years as well.

There are some other areas that will be seen in later chapters. The additional areas that I fall into and flip-flop would be substance abuse, and excessive spending while in a state of mania. Could these behaviors just be leading up to the next suicide attempt? Think about it. During these times, it could be easily considered that I was losing self-control. After all, is lost, it's time to check out.

Now in the fifth criteria which states one who has frequent attempts at suicidal behaviors, threats, gestures, and/or self-mutilating behavior. Self-mutilating behavior can be anything from cuts, scratches, intentional burns, hair pulling, head or wrist banging, to name a few. I have a lot of experience in this section of the nine criteria.

As mentioned before that I am a "cutter." I started cutting at sixteen and moved back and forth from burning myself with a Zippo, cigarette, or a metal wire (branding), and even biting myself. I've even chewed at my wrist while on suicide watch trying to get to my radial artery. I do many of these things for different reasons, but never to get attention like most textbooks say. My gestures have been in lengthy filled empathic suicide notes about me passing on and such. Other suicidal gestures have been used to manipulate people and family members to get my way for whatever it is that I may want. Same goes for the threats of suicide. Despite my use of threats, any attempt I have ever made was real, and I became very upset when I was found laying semi-conscious while the person(s) who had found me and gotten help right away, thus keeping me alive. They should have let me die in all truthfulness.

I have had eight serious suicide attempts. Some of them even landed me in the ICU. My first attempt was serious, and I didn't care if I lived or died, but all in all, I was proving a point to my then girlfriend's parents. Her name is Kelly, and my method was slitting of the wrists. She was also the first true love I ever had. Then I used a car, a garage, and carbon-monoxide poisoning.

There was an intentional pill overdose, where I took sixty-four red pills and lived. I tried this method again some months down the road. These were before I was eighteen. None during my military years except one time I put an unloaded 9mm in my mouth and pulled the trigger. A Sargent had seen me do this and completely flipped out, so then I was taken to the hospital to have a psychiatric evaluation. After my service, I had slit my wrists again (the right way this time), took an overdose of Valium, then Xanax a few months later. Furthermore, I used other prescription medication for about six months' worth which was a cocktail of Trazodone, Celexa, and Gabapentin. During most to all my attempts, I've ingested massive amounts of alcohol because one I knew that it would mix well and do more damage to my organs. Two, it was something I had to ingest as I didn't want to take the chance if there was an afterlife, but it had no booze in it. So, I wanted to load up while I could. That is a glimpse inside the mind of an alcoholic and his thinking.

A lot of people don't understand cutting, and if they don't understand something; then they become afraid of it. They may ask, but they truly never want the real answer people like me may give. When I cut, I get a release of my sense of self. Seeing the blood run down my arm turning bright red is something that can feel so surreal and like I've stepped outside of myself to watch the blood run cold. This can be a form of disassociation. There are still many reasons why I self-injure, which you'll see in later chapters.

The sixth criteria are when one has a marked instability due to moods, such as irritability, anxiety, and intense episodic dysphoria. Borderline personality has once been called the women's syndrome. I think these criteria is where they got that nickname, while a borderline has such a constant shifting of moods, like the stereotypical description of a woman. When a man hears this though it can become quite confusing as to thinking, "Did they just diagnose me with a condition meant for women?" Moreover, BPD has also been called the wastebasket syndrome. Just think how someone with this condition would feel if they knew the nickname for BPD was wastebasket syndrome.

The wastebasket syndrome comes from the borderline meeting some of the criteria for Dissociative Identity Disorder, DID, Bipolar, and Schizophrenia, but not enough for one of those diagnoses. They came up with BPD, Borderline Personality Disorder. Hints the wastebasket syndrome, just grabbing a little from each diagnosis.

I hate to use the word unstable, but that pretty much describes me according to my mood. My mother once described me to a doctor as having to walk on eggs shells when around me. That is a hallmark saying when describing borderlines. What that means is one minute or even one second I'd be fine and then, bam I'd blow up at her for pretty much any tiny little thing. I remember her always saying to me when I was a teen, "What did I do?" or I'd end up falling into a black depression of hopelessness and will to live. Not to mention my freak-outs about nothing when having an anxiety or panic attack, but these would not last very long, and I'd go back to normal without any reason. As you can see borderlines can be very confusing for people to deal with (just pointing it out one more time).

Even most psychologists and therapists will only take on one or two borderlines on their caseload due to the person's excessive neediness, outrageous demands, and how time-consuming a borderline can be to treat, but there are some clinicians who specialize in treating borderlines so they will have more of them on their caseload. As a teen when I was in therapy I went through more than a handful of therapists. One constantly passing me off to a colleague, and then that person would pass me off to another colleague. I came to think that they were playing a game of "Hot Potato" with me. It was as if they said this kid is impossible to work with so here why don't you try, because I don't have to deal with this type of shit from him (that's me, him). I believe the reason why they all refused to work with me was due to my hostility towards them, and how my ever-changing mood in their office made their job difficult to do, plus I constantly threatened them with harm and reminded them of how much smarter I was then they were, which I was. Even now in my life I still felt empty on the inside while battling an invisible enemy of mine and not knowing how to beat it. Hints the pain that turns to anger, and then the anger turns to threats followed by actions.

The seventh criteria say that a borderline will have chronic feelings of emptiness. These criteria suit me to a tee. At sixteen when I lost Katy and Jeremy in my life it was as if a huge hole was ripped out of my heart. After their deaths, I never felt right again. My body was empty on the inside, just like a hollow shell of nothingness. This is another reason why I cut myself. After I make the slash across my arm I can see my skin open like a fish being filleted, and as I see the wound open up and watching for a second or two before the blood comes running out of me. I feel the warmth of the blood running down my arm; only then do I know that my body is still alive on the inside and not hollow or empty. Human blood is the life source of us. Sometimes I cut just out of sheer boredom too. That's kind of a scary thought huh, someone who is bored so the activity they choose is to cut on themselves. This is a dangerous activity to do period, and I do engage in it when I'm just bored; it could become quite deadly one day if I cut the wrong artery.

Depending on what book you look at in these criteria besides the chronic feeling of emptiness it also states that one would have huge feelings of boredom along with the emptiness. Despite having lived a reckless and crazy life I am constantly bored with my life. For example, I could finish reading the most fascinating book and the second I finish it and close it shut. I'd be right back to feel board out of my mind. I feel therefore I constantly need the stimulation of excitement whether that be driving fast or a hot and heavy one night stand, or maybe even spending money I don't have just for the sheer joy of buying something expensive. If I can't do any of those things I could end up cutting myself, because I can't find anything stimulating to do, but the rush of slashing myself open tends to do the trick when all else fails. Cutting can also release my need for anger when I become enraged, or I use it as a tool for self-punishment.

The eight criteria states a borderline has difficulty or inappropriate anger or difficulty controlling anger. In addition to frequent displays of tempter, re-occurrent fights, and constant anger. This suits me to a tee once again.

People who have known me for any part of my life would say I have anger issues. My anger can range from mild, which could be a verbal tongue lashing to the person on the receiving end or to the point of throwing objects. Sometimes I turn my anger upon myself, which usually comes in the form of "cutting" or something along those lines. Not to mention the fights during my mid to late teens and into my twenties especially during my military years. At that time, we were getting into bar fights or fighting amongst ourselves. My tempers had been difficult to control or manage in my life, but one would describe them as the St. Louis whether; if you don't like the current weather (my temper) wait five minutes and it may change. Moreover, in my teens, I played ice hockey and at the levels, I was playing at we would take off our helmets and dropped the gloves, fighting just like how they do in the pros. Think about that for a minute.

In my teens, I played a sport if you wanted to fight someone all you had to do is grab them and, "Fights on!" Then I enter the Army at eighteen and for one we were being trained to fight and kill, but we were fighting amongst ourselves also. Those fights were more like the fights of brothers having it out with each other over a disagreement. Don't forget about the bar fights too. The point is starting in my mid-teens into my twenties I was surrounded by testosterone where fighting was condoned. These environments would be the perfect mask since borderline disorder comes on about in late teens to early adulthood. Thus, making the people who surrounded me in life that they would think the excessive fighting was all part of the sport or occupation. Onto the ninth and last criteria.

The last criteria states a person who would fall into the borderline diagnoses would have, "transient, stress-related paranoid ideation or severe dissociative symptoms". As I noted earlier I don't feel that I meet these criteria so I will leave this one alone. And none of my psychologists has ever mentioned these criteria to me when speaking about my condition.

As you may see that I meet eight of the nine criteria when only five are necessary. This more than qualifies me for the diagnosis. I listed this one first because that seems to be the front-runner amongst all my other diagnoses. Next, I'll tackle Bipolar disorder.

Bipolar disorder is defined by its key characteristic which is extreme mood swings, from manic highs to severe depression (lows) according to the Bipolar Disorder Survival Guide by Dr. Miklowitz. This disorder is called a mood disorder because it affects a person's experience of emotion and "affect" (the way one would convey their emotions to others.) For example, if someone came up to me to inform me that my sister was in a bad car accident, and I starting laughing instead of showing shocked and concerned emotion to the person who informed me of the tragic news. Basically, it's when a person shows inappropriate emotions (affect) for any given situation.

People with bipolar disorder have experiences of manic and depressive episodes. A few examples would be roller-coaster mood states (euphoria, irritability, and depression), changes in energy or activity levels, changes in thinking and perception, suicidal thoughts, sleeping issues, and impulsive or self-destructive behavior. As you might see a lot of the symptoms with bipolar disorder overlap with the ones for borderline personality disorder, but I've been told that they can be both diagnosed together for one person, not just one or the other.

The criteria listed below is the same for Bipolar II except for with Bipolar I an individual experiences a full manic episode. The criteria for bipolar disorder according to the DSM-IV (TR) are as follows:

A.) Presence (or history) of one or more Major Depressive Episodes.

B.) Presence (or history) of at least one Hypomanic Episode (highs).

C.) There has never been a Manic Episode or a Mixed Episode.

D.) The mood symptoms in criteria A and B are not better accounted for by Schizoaffective Disorder and are not superimposed on Schizophrenia, Schizophreniform Disorder, Delusional Disorder, or Psychotic Disorder Not Other Specified.

E.) The symptoms cause clinically significant distress or impairment in social, occupational, or other areas of functioning.

Some of my depressive episodes would look like me having a complete loss of energy. There would be times when I could barely get out of bed, while things felt hopeless to me. I would be so depressed that despite wanting to die/commit suicide; I just didn't have the energy to carry a plan through. Even doing a simple load of laundry felt like working a complicated physics problem. I isolated myself from my friends, ignoring their invites to events and such. It felt like I was laying on my bed, and I had a thousand-pound weight on me, which I was unable to move from under that burdensome weight. Nothing mattered in my life. If I managed to get out of bed I walked around with a big black storm cloud looming over my head, following me around like a lost puppy. When depression grabs ahold of you it's as if you are fighting, a heavy current trying to swim upstream against it until you finally give in and stop trying. That's when all your energy has abandoned you, and you have lost the battle to depression.

There is a saying about high blood pressure being the silent killer because you could have high blood pressure and not know it until something bad happens. I feel depression should be added to that saying because depression will take your life away once it hits. Meaning one who becomes depressed will lose interest in all things he/she had enjoyed in the past, become distant from one's friends, and more until all is lost. By that point, no one would know when suicidal plans start to come into play. Then bam, you're dead.

In describing one of my manic episodes would be reckless spending such as opening a web business while spending over one-thousand dollars to start it, and then closing it 48 hours later because I hadn't made thousands of thousands of dollars in those two days. Or spending fifteen hundred dollars in two days or so on expensive watches: Bolivia, Seiko, Citizen, or Steiger. At those times my ideas were racing so fast that all of them seemed like the best idea ever. On that same note, I'd not be fully thinking my decisions out either. I've experienced euphoria during these times as well. It's like floating ten feet above others, feeling delighted all over. Lastly, to touch on my energy levels would be described as upped, and I was willing to go out and do anything or go anywhere; I'd constantly be calling people at all hours to find some additional adventures to go on. My friends weren't too happy about the middle of the night phone calls either.

When looking at the criteria I meet both A and B. My symptoms do not fall into the criteria of section D. The last section states about the symptoms of Bipolar disorder having clinically impaired in the following areas: with significant distress in social, occupational, or other important areas of functioning.

As I listed above in both my depressive and manic episodes one can see where they affect my work/job while having a flight of ideas and racing thoughts while trying to communicate with patients when I worked in a doctor's office. In addition, while in manic states it has affected my social circle of friends by calling them at all hours trying to begin a new adventure, and at the same time having grandiose thinking, which puts my own personal thoughts and actions above others as they would be the ultimate ideas. Doctors say that while in a manic episode's patients often deny that they are having any current symptoms. Manic episodes are very euphoric and while I experience them I feel good, so good to the point I would be fine staying in one while refusing help. During these times, I am not open to hearing anybody who tells me that something is wrong and that I should seek help. Why would I seek such help when I am feeling incredible? They call me Superman. Some people will even skip their medications to bring on a manic episode just to re-experience the euphoria. There is another symptom which is irritability. I experience this as well, and that can also push people away in the same sense. Furthermore, my irritability while at work can have a major effect on my job while working with other staff and patients. I would become extremely short with them often having complaints called in about me.

I've also experienced what is called pressured speech. It would come on when I am extremely irritated or overwhelmed with a flood of emotions. My speech would become so pressured that I developed a stuttering problem. As you can see how this would affect my work with patients, co-workers, and friends in my social circle. On the opposite side of that, you have the depressive episodes.

The symptoms are pretty much the opposite. I'd push friends away, alienating and isolating from them, because I just wouldn't have the energy to even move or deal with anybody. There would be times it would be such a chore to even have a phone conversation for me. Lastly, during my depressive episode, my sleep would become increased to the point one may think I am dead due to my lack of movement. I've been in more depressive states than manic ones over the course of my life.

When you put all this together one ends up with a diagnosis of Bipolar disorder, which is my second diagnosis. Keep in mind there are a lot of different pathways that a patient can display to be diagnosed with Bipolar disorder. Up next will be my discussion of my OCD Traits.

Obsessive-Compulsive Disorder is defined as an anxiety disorder involving unwanted, persistent, intrusive thoughts and impulses as well as repetitive actions intended to suppress them, according to the Abnormal Psychology textbook written by Barlow and Durand, fourth edition. People with OCD are likely to experience severe generalized anxiety, often panic attacks, and major depression; all these symptoms can co-occur along with the obsessive-compulsive symptoms. People with OCD are often hospitalized for the active symptoms for a period of time. According to Barlow and Durand, "Obsessions are intrusive and mostly nonsensical thoughts, images, or urges that the individual tries to resist or eliminate." In addition, "Compulsions are the thoughts or actions used to suppress the obsessions and provide relief."

People with OCD have a need for symmetry, contamination prevention, aggressive impulses, and sexual content. The need for symmetry would be keeping things balanced and in perfect order, but it must be a certain way too. Compulsions would be an example of what is called, "Checking Rituals." These rituals are used to serve as a purpose to prevent an imagined disaster or catastrophe. The mental act of "counting" could be considered a compulsion. Some of my obsessions are focusing on only one aspect of something leaving out the rest until the point of what I was focusing on falls by the wayside along with everything else.

I tend to have more on the side of compulsions than anything else. I am what one would call a "checker" and "counter". I'm constantly checking and re-checking my car door locks, and the locks to my house. Then I re-check them all over again, just to make sure to prevent a tragedy from happening. This can be repeated several times over. I have a strong need for symmetry in my life. My books, DVDs, and all my nick-knacks should be a certain way, and I'm completely inflexible on this too. In order to make sure they are safe I count them numerous times throughout the day. Furthermore, I don't like people to touch my things either. For example, my doctor's office was being remodeled and we had to work out of a different office for a few months. When I brought all my office stuff down with me I completely lost it, because I couldn't set it up exactly how it was in the original office. Then months later when we moved back I thought I would have some relief. No, that did not happen, because my counter space had been changed and guess what happened? I completely lost it once again. Even the pillows on my bed (I have eight of them) are only arranged in one way. I wouldn't do well mentally if one went missing or was taken away. There is even more symmetry that I desire in my life down to my entire room, such as it should be organized in a very functional way, in addition, to me even just checking, re-checking my room and checking again one more time to make sure the room is okay. I know this sounds ridiculous, but it's something I should do to have peace. It's kind of hard to describe because there is just a feeling that comes over me that things should be just right, like Goldilocks and the Three Bears or the big bad wolf will come and take it all way. This causes much anxiety in my life, especially living in fear that if things aren't just right something bad will happen. Not to mention my excessive counting of items that I count through-out the day. (E.g. chairs, people, DVDs, car spaces, etc.)

I have some of the characteristics for a partial diagnosis of an Obsessive-Compulsive Disorder. Hints the traits. OCD also can be diagnosed with an Obsessive-Compulsive Personality disorder (OCPD). OCPD is described as characterized by a fixation on things being done the "right way". While this sounds like a great character trait for workers; they become preoccupied with details which prevents them from completing much of anything. People with this trait could be considered "masters of control," because of their need to have everything their way. There are eight different criteria for OCPD, which are: 1.) Preoccupied with details, rules, lists, order, organization, or schedules to the extent that the major point of the activity is lost. I am very detailed oriented as I make lists and keep things in order. I'm beyond what a person would call as organized because every little detail in my life is organized and in order. I pretty much want one calls a control freak. 3.) States one is excessively devoted to work and productivity to the exclusions of leisure activities and friendships. This is me too. I've always given more than I could at work than others, which bosses saw, but I lost out on a social life as well. 4.) Is over conscientious, scrupulous, and inflexible about matters of morality, ethics, or values. I get into constant debates with people about many issues, but I never give in no matter what. I'll debate you till your blue in the face. 6.) States one is reluctant to delegate tasks or to work with others unless they submit to exactly his or her way of doing things. This is the only way I work, plus I don't see a point in delegating, because if you want anything done right you better do it yourself. 8.) Says the person shows rigidity and stubbornness. Again, I am a very stubborn person when it comes to most all of things, and I will debate someone till the end of time just to win, even if I know I am wrong. All of this shows much rigidity in myself and my life. Even as a teen I had a very organized routine and life, which worked out great for my time in the military. Another example of where my mental illnesses were hidden due to my lifestyle.

I have never been diagnosed with OPCD, but I do feel that it fits me more accurately. You may have noticed that some of the numbers were missing in the 8 total, but I chose to list the criteria that pertain to me, Matthew. Either way, these do overlap with some similar symptoms. So, you can call it to me either having the traits of OCD or OCPD. The main point is these symptoms affect my daily life, but I only have some, and I do not qualify for a full diagnosis of them either, just traits. Who is more self-obsessed then me.

        The narcissistic personality disorder is defined, "as a person involving a pervasive pattern of grandiosity in fantasy or behavior, need for admiration, and a lack of empathy," according to the textbook written together by Barlow and Durand. In describing the narcissistic personality, a person will have an unreasonable sense of self and self-importance. Often exaggerating their own abilities, while having the need for constant attention and admiration. These people lack sensitivity and compassion for others as well. When one experiences exaggerated feelings and their fantasies of greatness that is called grandiosity. Lastly, the narcissistic personality expects great deals of attention while also expecting special treatment for all situations, such as being a permanent VIP person in everyday life.

According to the DSM-IV (TR), there are nine criteria that one needs to meet five or more of the criteria listed as follows:

1.) Has a grandiose sense of self-importance (e.g. exaggerates achievements and talents, expects to be recognized as superior with commensurate achievements).

2.) Is preoccupied with fantasies of unlimited success, power, brilliance, beauty, or ideal love.

3.) Believes he/she is "special" and unique and can only be understood by, or should associate with, other special or high-status people (or institutions).

4.) Requests excessive admiration.

5.) Has a sense of entitlement, i.e., unreasonable expectations of especially favorable treatment or automatic compliance with his/her expectations.

6.) Is interpersonally exploitative i.e. takes advantage of others to achieve his/her own ends.

7.) Lacks empathy; is unwilling to recognized or identify with the feelings and needs of others.

8.) Is often envious of others or believes that others are envious of him/her.

9.) Shows arrogant, haughty behaviors or attitudes.

I wonder if someone got a diagnosis of narcissism and understood what that meant. Would they be proud of the diagnoses or not? I have a great lack of empathy for others, just because I don't care for people in general. I find them rather trivial and boring with their pathetic little lives. Moreover, borderlines too lack some empathy. I believe our society is becoming more narcissistic every day with Tweeting, Facebooking, and all that other crap they do on social media. Your tweets and status updates are not newsworthy. Do other people care what you have to say? Not really, in my opinion. People are objects just like pawns on a chess board. I think the only another thing I care for is my doggie, Mr. Houdini, and my 2011 BMW; I call her Lucy.

People might exaggerate a story now and then, but would someone exaggerate all of them? I do. For example, when I switched from playing defense in hockey to right wing my goal scoring seemed to be the highest in the league when it was most likely average. Then you have some of my cars that I no longer own, and I'd tell people how much money I had put into them to make them faster, and look better, such as my Honda Civic, which I paid around seven thousand dollars for in 2001, but I tell people I put over thirty thousand into it when it was more like eight or nine hundred. My reasons for this is because I must prove to people how much better I am then they are. Hints on how someone would come to admire me, want to be me, and have my car.

I often daydream about my own success that would put me above the population of the people of Earth. I'm sure peoples' parents told them that they were "special" little beings when they were younger, but mine just slapped me around and told me I would never be good enough for anything. I disagreed as a teenager, and as I entered adulthood. My personal thoughts were of that I would not be nameless, faceless, and that I was born for greatness, nor would I be lost in a sea of faces. I long for admiration and constantly have the need to be envied as I am much better than all the average people out there. This also applies to my intelligence over others as I use it to insult most people when I talk down to them, or I treat them as if I am speaking to a child. If you have the skill, why not use it to put yourself above others who are not as smart as you. In the same note, I often found myself very envious of others, especially college graduates, but from the way I talk to them I make them envious of me in return, because I am better than they are and smarter too.

Since having come to terms with my mental illnesses I command of others that they must treat me with "kid" gloves as in not to piss me off otherwise they would receive my verbal tongue lashing unleashed upon them. I expect when I go to places like my doctor's office that I do not wait and am treated with over exceptional care. I intend not to ever be confronted, and that all people treat me with the tactical care of any issues that may cause problems for me mentally and if not look out.

As one can see that I fall into some of the diagnostic criteria for Narcissistic personality disorder. The question is am I proud of this or not? I believe I don't meet five or more of the criteria, and that leaves me with the partial diagnosis of Narcissistic personality disorder, thus leaving me with having narcissistic traits.

These are all my substance abuse and mental health diagnoses. The doctors who wrote, "I Hate You, Don't Leave Me", also wrote a follow-up book called, "Sometimes I Act Crazy, Living with Borderline Personality Disorder." And sometimes I just might act crazy, despite the fact I do not like that word "crazy", but I'll cover that in a later chapter. So, let's begin with what one would call my crazy life, and who fucked me up in the head in the first place and where.

Chapter 3: The Childhood Years

I am born into this world, but I never asked to be. Matthew's life begins. I often tell people that I do not remember all or any parts of my childhood. That way I don't have to discuss it with them. Now I am discussing those memories here for the first time, well some of them. I remember as a teen my family showing me pictures of me when we went to Florida and crap like that. My true thoughts are when shown these pictures is how do I know that that is me in those pictures. It could be an imposter. This is one way I deny my painful childhood memories. Who wants to remember those crappy times anyhow? My parents may say that I had so much fun during those times, but I don't remember much of it, or why should I accept this information at face value if I was never there. There are parts of it I do remember though, and those are painful memories.

Most psychologists will agree that diagnosing a child is difficult because they are not yet grown, especially with personality disorders. Many personality disorders are diagnosed in late adolescence and early adulthood. I'm sure there were some hallmark signs that there were things wrong with me from the beginning. And it was not just the death of my friends in high school that kicked off my mental illnesses. Like most people think.

When I was about eight or nine I became curious about the opposite sex. That year was also the year I saw my first vagina in the flesh. It was an amazing thing to see. It was a family friend who was of the same age as me. Her name will be called Lisa. I do remember that on our trips to Florida we stayed with these people in a nice condo that was close to the beach, and it also had a pool right out front. Lisa and I would kiss and whatnot in a back bedroom or closet, so no one would find us. One time while in Florida we all went out and played mini-golf. Later, that night when we arrived back at the condo Lisa and I played a game of strip mini-golf out on the balcony. I'm not sure how this idea of strip mini-golf came about. We would also mess around at her house whenever our family went over there to visit. I'm not sure where my desire to see the opposite sexes body came from, but I developed that curiosity early on in my life.

I had an older neighbor who lived across the street from me and it was Peter's sister. She was about two or three years older than me. I had to be around ten or so. I made her an offer for me to see hers, and she could see mine too. After some negotiation, we decided to go behind my red brick house over by a big green bush of a tree that was right by my bedroom window to handle the showing of private areas, which one would think all kids do this at some point in time. Curiosity and all. My curiosity extended to multiple girls at multiple times. It's like my sex drive started at seven-ish or something, and it was high. Or something had to have happened to me that I don't remember.

When I was much younger, about six or seven maybe. I was attending a work party thing for my mother. I remember it being outside, and it had lots of things to do and tents set up for actives; there was even a fire-truck with fireman there too. I have a picture of this time. The picture is of me with my white curly blonde hair kissing some girl my age. One of us is holding a red balloon, which is right in between us. We even had our eyes closed. I don't remember her name but I'm sure I knew it back then. She was also a blonde too, like me, except she had a blue ribbon in her hair which, matched my blue shirt. I do not know who the girl was, but I still have kept that picture to this day. I often wonder what became of this girl? Did she go off to college and became a success, is she married, or has she ended up with a troubled life, like mine. I think it would be neat to be able to find this lady and meet her, but that is very unlikely.

The reason why I remember this day so much is because of what happened with the fireman. Plus, the picture I have of this mystery girl and me. It all happened on that same warm sunny day. I still have that picture of her and me to this very day some twenty-eight years later.

As I was playing and enjoying myself around the festivities when I found myself engaged in a conversation with a fireman. He told me that on his fire-truck he had a machine that could take a picture of my heart. I thought that was cool. Then he asked me if I wanted to get a picture of my heart taken. I said, "Yes", and followed him to the truck. There he had me take off my shirt as he got the machine out. I'm not one-hundred percent sure what happened next, because I lost time during that moment. I remember suddenly the fireman tells me that his heart machine has no film in it and that he couldn't take the picture. Things became a blur for me then and before I know it was a few days later. Did something happen with the fireman or not; I'm not sure, but after that year I had a much-increased need to see girls I met naked. Whether that event sparked my sex interest or not I do not know. I've never told anybody about this event until now.

A few years later I am about ten or eleven, and I had a babysitter named Emma. She was the last babysitter I had because after her I was told I was too old for sitters or so my parents thought so. I did have other sitters before her, and I remember always wanting them to be gorgeous ones at that, and if not I would complain about them until my parents found someone prettier. One time my parents had a guy sitter come over, which did not sit well with me. By the end of that night, he ended up ducted tapped and tied. I had placed duct-taped across the lower portion of a doorway, and I called this male babysitter. When he came into the room he tripped on the tape, and I attacked. After I was done with him he was tied with twisted tape. I did that because I knew it would be harder to break, and I had his mouth taped shut too. When my parents arrived home and saw the sitter tied up there was the look of utter shock on their faces, and it was priceless. My parents untied the sitter, and he vowed never to come back again. My next sitter was a pretty lady named Emma.

It's late one night and Emma is babysitting me. I manage to talk her into a game of strip poker. Nothing happened, but we played a few hands, and I cheated my butt off to get her to remove some of her clothes. I believe she knew I was cheating, but she allowed me to win and her clothes came off. Where did such a curiosity for sex come out of me at such a young age, I don't know, but it was there. Could this have been the start of my screwed-up psyche?

As a little tike, I often got into all kinds of trouble. Though not the trouble one would first think of when reading that. I have had many head injuries as a tiny boy. The first one I am aware of is when I was jumping up and down on my bed. The bed was just a mattress that was held up by cinder blocks. Big grey ones. I managed to fall off the bed, and the back of my head went smack on the grey cinder block. Thus, splitting my head right open, while my blood came gushing out. One of my parents took me to the emergency room. There they put in some stitches, and I was all better. The second or third time I split my head open was when I was playing with my sister who shoved me into the corner of the wall that intersects between the hallway and the living room, which is decorated eighties style since it was the eighties. Those are the two times I remember splitting my tiny head open, but I have a total of four to five scars in the back of my head, so I don't remember all the times. The scars have the accurate count though. My head injuries were when I was between the ages of say five and eight. Whether my childhood head injuries affected my overall psyche when I grew older is up for debate, because some psychologists say head injuries at such a young age can affect the psyche at a much later time. I did grow up to be a very organized kid though.

I was always a neat and tidy kid. I can remember having a clean room; a room so clean that it would pass a military white glove inspection. This is something I went through years later, while in the Army. I always passed the white glove inspections. Everything was in a special order, while all things would be aligned and perfect. Here is where my need for symmetry begins. Even my clothes were in order down to my sock drawer, and they still are to this very day. All my socks were balled up and lined next to one another like little soldiers waiting for orders. In addition, my shirts would be hanging in color-coordinated order and pants matching by color and style.

One time after watching an episode of Full House I saw where Danny Tanner (Bob Sagat) had his clothes labeled on a hanger. All his outfits were assigned for a specific day of the week. I thought this was just the best idea ever! I began to label my outfits for the week in a similar manner. One of my favorite things to do besides play ice hockey was to re-arrange my room.

I could spend hours moving things around trying to get everything "just right." I believe this was the start of my OCD traits forming during my screwed-up childhood. I had similar organizational bouts with my hockey equipment. Everything had a place and there was a place for everything. If something went out of its place I lost my mind, or if the original place was taken up by something else that didn't belong there, again I would lose it.

Losing it is like when everything in your head was once organized and it then, "losing it" is as if it is all shaken up. Things ordered become disordered. It hard to reassemble everything back into that, "right place." There is panic, confusion, and a jumbled mind to compete against. This time is very unsettling.

In the third grade, I was awarded the "Dino-Cleano" award, but I was a shoe-in for it. The award should have been called the OCD award. Every week Mrs. Tewell would inspect our desks and the person's desk who was the cleanest and most organized would be the winner of the Dino-Cleano award for the week. They would be then given a purple dinosaur to hold onto for the week. This would go on for the entire year, and at the end of the year, she would award the person who had the Dino-Cleano dinosaur the most would be given a special certificate as getting the Dino-Cleano Award for the year. I bet you can guess who got it the year I was in the third grade. Yep, it was me. Surprised? My need for symmetry and organization at home carried right on through to my desk at school. Even my hockey equipment was organized.

I began playing hockey as a young child. I was between nine and ten when I started. My reason for wanting to play this sport was because I saw the NHL players playing a game one night and found out that they would travel from state to state to play other teams. The team I watched that night was the St. Louis Blues. My parents signed me up after I manipulated them into letting me play hockey with my high-quality verbal skills at selling myself to them for me to play the sport. Those skills came helpful much later in life as I used them in many ways to manipulate people.

So, my first year of hockey was on a "learn to play" team, which is called Mite (House). Here we did not travel. I was upset to find this out. So, I asked my father how come my team didn't play like the NHL players did. He explained to me that you must be the best of the best of the best to play at those levels. At that time the best level for me to play at was double A (AA). Eventually, AA did do some traveling when I was older. I built up a gigantic love for this sport and desire to play in the NHL. My father told me it would be very unlikely that I ever would make it to the NHL; he gave me the odds of someone making it into the NHL, and how truly hard one would have to work to play at that level, but the odds were still slim to none. He did not give me much positive encouragement to continue with my dream, but I got started anyway. I figured if my hard work would pay off then there is a fighting chance in hell I would make it into the NHL.

I put in the work needed to move up my level of play or skill level. And that is what happened. Within a year or two I was playing at the AA level and doing some traveling. Besides practicing with my team, I put in the work off the ice as well. That included running and working out to build up my strength. Keep in mind I am still in grade school at this time, about eleven or twelve. My skill level was being noticed by people and coaches I'd never met before. The St. Louis triple A (AAA) Blues team had noticed me, and I was invited to try-out. That is the only way to play on a team like this is by invitation only. This team traveled out of state every other weekend like the Pros, except the players weren't paid to play like the NHL guys were. The AA team only traveled out of state for some tournaments. So, I had tried out, but my first time out I didn't make the team. There was more work to be done.

I wouldn't say I experienced much physical abuse from my father, but it was the eighties, so I looked at that as how things were done back then, not to mention he was also an alcoholic. My father would constantly scold me for not being good enough while grabbing me with force. This went on for the duration of my childhood years while trying to improve my skill level at hockey. During this time, I was sent off to hockey camp for two summers in Minnesota.

The camp I attended was Steve Jensen's Heartland Hockey Camp. Here I was in Minnesota away from that god-awful city called St. Louis, and I was alone and on my own. I learned many new skills, and I even picked up some new training exercises, such as putting Plexiglass down in the driveway and shooting real hockey pucks at a regulation goal. This simulates shooting a puck off the ice without the expense of having to buy ice time as that was quite costly per hour.

When I arrived home, I was able to ask my father to get ahold of some Plexiglass and a real hockey net. He built a regulation goal for me, and I could start improving my shot while off the ice and that I did. At the end of the day, my father would ask me, "How much time did you spend outside working on your shot?" I would usually reply that I was out there for about an hour or so. He would explode into a rage and yell at me while telling me that an hour won't get me into the pros. He would often force me back out there for many more hours. In a way, I guess this is what one kid would need to get on the pro level track. Constantly being pushed past regular limits and so forth. This was something I went through until age 16/17. Eventually, I would go onto teaching at hockey camps when I was fifteen, and sometimes I taught other players my age or older. At fifteen while working for many different camps and hockey schools it showed how my developed skills were above others that were my age and above. This was a great sign that I was moving along the right track to make it to the NHL. I hardly knew any coach that asked me to teach at a camp; coaches just knew me by my level of play while standing out during my games.

There was verbal and emotional abuse going on as my father tried to push my level of play up, and it did go up both the verbal abuse and emotional abuse, along with my level of play. I guess I should be grateful for this, but (spoiler alert) I quit playing hockey by eight-teen. There were other times when he'd grab my stomach and called me fat while in a rage, pointing out what cellulite was. I may have been a chubby child, but I thinned out as I grew during adolescence. I have always struggled with my weight since these times, by making sure it was on the lower side of normal. It got to the point where when I was older I became very vain having to skip meals while making sure I looked good with my shirt off, but that comes on down the line a bit. Due to the ways, my father treated me during my childhood I never felt like I could go and speak to him like a son, nor did I ever go to him for advice on girlfriend issues and such. He was lost to me as a father. When I wasn't practicing my hockey skills, I was quite the little thief.

My neighbor Victor and I organized our own theft ring. We were between the ages of ten and twelve. We would go into Walgreens and steal them, "Good School Supplies." It's not like our parents couldn't afford the supplies we wanted, but we took them from the store anyway. Victor and I would go into the store and steal the fancy notebooks, and mechanical pencils and what not. We often sold them to other kids whose parents refused to buy them the fancy supplies. We would stick the loot down the arms of out flight jackets, and we would put things in our waistline. The last year we stole from the store was when my parents asked me what I needed for school, and I replied that I was good. As I already had my supplies. My parents were never onto our theft ring, but I believe we just got burnt out of stealing from the store, in addition, the rush of stealing had left just and it got boring. That wasn't the first time I robbed Walgreens though. I did steal a toy hotrod from there, but I confessed my sins when I got home to my mother. I was about six at that time. I guess I needed some practice for what was to come. Victor was one of my neighborhood friends along with a few other kids.

There was Peter, Jenni, Victor, and Brad. These were my childhood friends. Brad lived in a different part of town, but his grandmother lived on our street a couple of houses up, and he was over there visiting quite often. His grandmother had this grey little poodle, but I don't remember its name. Here I go, I'm a little kid, and I have some neighborhood friends like most childhood kids do. Or one might think they are my friends because there were plenty of events where I went beyond pushing them away to outright scaring them away.

I don't remember what Peter that day did to piss me off, but one time I ran inside my home to get a steak knife to stab him. I never did stab Peter that day, but I did get the knife and chased him in hopes of catching him and stabbing him while I wanted to cause much harm to him. I remember chasing Peter on that summer day. When I flew out my front door, he took off. Peter shifted and spun about as I follow with my feet slipping on the grass as I shifted directions. Then as my shoe slipped away my knee would hit the ground, and I would spring off the ground lurching forward towards Peter. This would go on until one or both of us became tire and then the episode would subside. This episode was most likely a very small thing he did that set me off. All I remember thinking was how much I wanted to hurt Peter that day and cause him bodily harm. It's as if my mind went into tunnel vision. Then there was the hockey stick incident.

One winter it snowed plentiful in my neighborhood. The snow-covered ground iced over on the pearl white snow in our yards and driveways. We got together that morning and bundled ourselves up to go out and play a game of hockey on our frozen yards that allowed us to slide around just like in an ice rink. Again, Peter had done something, most likely very minor to make me mad. So, I attacked. This time I don't have to get a steak knife; I have the hockey stick instead. There is at least a good four-foot range with a hockey stick. I still remember the stick. It was light blue with black lettering down the side and a white background behind that. As Peter moved past me I hauled off and did a two-handed baseball style swing right into the middle of his back with my blue stick in complete disregard for him and his safety. He yells out in pain.

I'm sure I voiced my reason for the attack after that, but all the kids out there playing were confused why would I do such a thing like that. Obviously, the game was over after that. To tell the truth today I don't remember why I did that beside the point that he pissed me off. Friends often didn't stay with me for very long. Was I a little sociopath in the making or did I have some other wires lose in my head?

These were not only the times I attacked the neighbor kids either. There were many more steak knife incidents with my other neighborhood friends like Victor and Brad. What I find strange is that as I went through my screen door, through the eighties style living room, and into the kitchen I knew not to grab the butter knife as it would do no damage. The steak knife had the serrated edge, I knew that was the ultimate choice of weapon. Not to mention that the pointed edge would go into the human body much better, like butter. I can still hear the clanking of utensils as I pulled the drawer open vigorously and grabbed that faded brown handle feeling the smoothed hardness as the pointed steel blade protruded from the wooden handle. Then I would fly out of my house back through the eighties style living room and out the screen door. Why I had these thoughts is unknown to me. Could anyone see that something was wrong with me, and my thinking; I'm under twelve during these times. I wonder what a psychologist would say if he/she could speak to me during these episodes. Was my mental illness forming back then, or was I just born different? Like a Martian. Or was I a little sociopath in the making?

Thinking back on it now, I'm not sure what to make of it. It is a very confusing time as to why I as a child would behave in these manners without any instructions from others. What went wrong with me? Was I born defective like an item they recalled in the stores, except they forgot to recall the Matthew model? I have had these feelings all throughout my life. It's like I was born from Mars or some other planet just waiting to return home. Being a stranger in a strange land, not knowing what to make of myself, while not feeling right in this time and space, even in my own skin. I did ingest alcohol as a child, but not much though.

My parents have a picture of me as a youngster holding up a Bud Light bottle, whether they admit to me drinking any of it is up for debate. They also have a picture of me holding a lit cigarette too. Some parents, huh? I am like five or six in these pictures. As my father was an alcoholic during my childhood I remember taking beers from the fridge, and sips of almost empty Busch cans, not to mention my mother's wine coolers. It's not like his drunken self would notice anyway. I didn't know wine coolers had alcohol in them until my older sister (by one year) explained that to me. So, I began gulping those down too, in addition, they tasted a tad better. I doubt I ever got drunk during these times, but those times were the first-time alcohol had touched my lips, and it wouldn't be the last either.

I don't remember the moments when I physically took the booze from my parents, but I do remember where I drank it at. That would be in the far-left corner of their garage. The heavy garage door would be closed and the area dark as the day is night. I would sneak sips leaving the empties there as evidence to be found. I never was caught nor was I ever questioned about the empty Busch cans and wine coolers that were left in my special corner. They probably figured that they kept leaving empties in the garage. My parents were never the type of parents to check on me as I went about their house. Come to think of it I was never caught doing anything by my parents as a child. I'm not sure where my mother was at during these times, but my father was most likely passed out if it was by mid-day on a weekend.

He was a stock/commodities broker, so my father was often home by noon and drinking during the week. I remember getting off the school bus around 3 pm or whatever time school got out back then. I would walk laterally down the street one block, and then I'd turn left onto my street, Lanvale Drive. My house was half-way down on the left. It was a red brick house, with ugly brown awnings, eighties style. I would come in the door and within minutes my father would be drunk on beer, yelling at me to clean the house. I didn't understand why the rage the minute I got home, or the need to have the house cleaned so abruptly. My thoughts were, "Hey ass-hole you've been home for three hours or so. Why don't you clean the fucking house!" I was not strong enough to stand up to him then, so I just cleaned the house. The thing I never understood was why did he have to yell the minute I got home versus just asking me to straighten up the house. I would think it was most likely the alcohol that made him act like this, but even now as he has been sober for twenty plus years I can see a lot of his shortcomings and defects of character that are there without the alcohol through his sober years. My father only stayed in AA for about a year, but he has managed to stay sober since. He quit drinking when I was about eleven years old. But my drinking was just beginning to emerge in the coming years.

I attended grade school at the computer school. Kindergarten through fifth grade was on the lower level, but the Steager school was on the upper level, which was the six graders school. I always have been attracted to older women. In the second grade, I was very fond of our recess aids daughter who would have been about 3 to 4 years older than me. Furthermore, besides enjoying the company of older babysitters I often spent my time getting out of class to walk around the sixth-grade floor hitting on the older six graders. I even managed to embarrass one.

While I was roaming the six-grade floor I had taken notice of a beautiful six-grader coming out of the bathroom, her name would be Kate. She had a white trail of toilet paper coming off her foot. Being the nice guy that I am I pointed it out to her from across the way in front of everybody. Kate removed the paper, and she headed back to class. I took a shining to this nice young lady, which I spent about three years pursuing with no luck.

Besides hitting on the older women around me in school I was also bullied by two older boys towards the end of my grade school years. This is the old style of bullying too; not the kind that happens these days, such as getting harassed online and on Facebook until the victim takes their life. These two boys tormented me while on the school bus ride to school. Besides saying mean things to me; they often hit the back of my seat, head, and what not.

One day I come home from school, and my father wants to horseplay around. I had a bad day at school (the two bullies), and I don't feel like talking. Eventually, my father pulls it out of me and calls me a pussy. I don't understand. He explains to me that I'm a tough kid and get knocked around while playing hockey all the time. Furthermore, he says most bullies generally won't fight back, and that I should stand up to them on the bus. He reiterates that I should be the first to take a swing and to make sure that I hit them in the face. I respond by asking what happens if they hit me in the face first before I can finish my question my father slaps me hard across the face, and he says now you know how it feels. Deal with it! The next morning comes as the sun rises over the horizon.

I walk to the bus stop, and I am mildly siked up about my upcoming fight with the two imbeciles. The bus comes, and I climb up the three steps one would need to climb on to get onto the bus. I walk past all the green bus seats until I find mine. The bus barely gets thirty feet away from the bus stop before the moron twins start in. I instantly fly into a rage and jump up almost high enough to clear my seat. As I begin verbally unloading on them I also find myself pushing them back further and farther. While none of the bullies take a stand before I know it I have them cornered all the way to the back of the bus where the "Emergency Door" is. No aggression comes from them, and they begin to bargain with me. The bus driver hears the commotion and pulls the bus over to kick all three of us off the bus. I get off that ugly yellow bus not sure what I should do. Should I continue my violent torrent on them or just walk home. The two bullies get off the bus with me but go the other way. I'm lost on what to do now, so I walk home. My father is still at home and drives me to school that day. He told me that he was right and says to see how the outcome was a positive result for me.

The interesting thing I see here is no one cared that some bus driver kicked all three of us off the bus, in the middle of the road. No parents seemed to pick up on this with outrage. In concluding, what I learned from the experience is when attacking an enemy whether they be bullies from school or some other person I need to defend myself against is to attack them like a rabid pit bull that will never quit. This line of thinking caused problems later in life and worked when the need to overcome people I have issues with, nor would I back down. And my father never hit me again or tried to from this day forward. After this, I never abided by any of my family's rules. I was set free to rain my terror down upon this planet because I no longer respected any authority too.

I had one real date with my mother's coworker's daughter her name was Michelle. We were the same age, I think I was around 12 at this time. I noticed right away the

Michelle had a natural beauty to her with her long brown thick flowing hair. We went ice skating at the Webster Groves outdoor ice rink. It was a magical time. I thought to myself that Michelle was very pretty, and I liked her. I told all of the kids in my class that I had gone on this date with her.

We spent the night skating circles around the rink, held hands, and we enjoyed each other's company. I was very excited about our time spent together. We went on a second date this time at the indoor ice rink that Webster had just built. This date was a train wreck caused by me.

We are about 14 when we went on our second date. But in the teenage years it wasn't cool to go skating, normally we would hang around the rink and cause friendly trouble. Michelle expected to go skating like we did last time, but I guess I forgot to inform her of what we really were going to do at the rink on this special nite. Michelle didn't want to hang out and she wanted to skate. I ended up ignoring her and spent my time hanging out with my buddies. This did not please her at all.

I had ruined the entire night and didn't even realize it to the end. Once we arrived back at my mom's house she began to pack her bags immediately, stuffing her things into the bag with much force. That is when I realized I had ruined the date.

I often regret ruining this date. As I realized at a much later time, we could have continued to date and maybe had a real relationship. Not to mention now in the present Michelle is a knockout. A nine out of ten. So I am left with what could have been; in my thoughts. Often regretting my mistake on our second date.

My childhood is over, and I am twelve. Up next is my teenage years (adolescence) where the real trouble starts to begin. As if my childhood was a prerequisite course for the hell to come. Where did it all go wrong?

Chapter 4: The Teenage Years

It all went wrong here. If you could read my first psychiatric notes of my teenage years most of them start off as, "Matthew was a well-adjusted teen, until the death of his high school friends Jeremy and Katy." I know this because I have read the notes. I guess they didn't take an accurate childhood history, or I never bothered to tell them. I guess I always found the interviews quite trivial, furthermore, I believed that the psychologists taking my history never really cared about my answers. I kept them short and sweet. For one I never understood why my parents put me in therapy, so I didn't know how it was supposed to work. I'm thirteen years old and in junior high. The therapy years don't come along for a couple of years.

The seventh and eighth-grade years went well for me. I was excelling in my hockey career while playing at the AA level. At that time, I was playing a defensive position, which was the position I started out playing, eventually, I switched to right wing. We did a little bit of traveling for tournaments, which gave me exposure to out of state coaches. Coaches talk amongst themselves, which is how coaches I have never heard of began to talk about me. I was invited to try out for the AAA team in seventh grade, but I was not good enough, or I didn't make a big enough impression for the 1982 AAA team coaches. That was okay at that time because the AA team I played on was a winning team that season as the AAA 82 team lost most of their games. I did well in school that year, getting all A's.

I attended Hixson junior high school for my seventh and eighth-grade years. My grades were well; all A's and only a small amount of B's. I never remember doing any homework or major projects in junior high, but I do remember taking tests and getting A's. My classes just felt easy to me, and I barely remember having to try in them either. Moreover, my only focus during these two years was playing hockey. That was my life at the time. It was the time to be noticed and move forward otherwise my hockey path would end with my senior year of high school, and I did not want that to happen as I felt I could go much further with my talents. I did have a focus on girls too.

During my junior high years, I had a handful of girlfriends, along with a handful of friends. All my male friends were fellow hockey players who were on my AA team. We would spend every waking hour messing around on the roller rink, while our group of girls watched us play. If we weren't playing there we could be found in the Webster Groves Ice rink right next store, playing pickup games. The thing is that we did not have the money to purchase ice time as kids, but since we were known as, "Rink Rats" we were able to convince either the ice rink manager or maintenance man to stay after the rink was closed, so we could skate on the ice. Sometimes we bribed these guys with cash for the beer that they could drink while we played. We often played until one or two in the morning. During the day we got ice time know as dead ice, which means the ice was rented and open for us rink rats to skate on. There would be times when our group of girls would watch us play on the ice late into the night, or they would come by and pick us up to hang out much later into the night. Our parents never seemed to mind since we were at the ice rink during these twilight hours.

When we weren't playing hockey in junior high our group would be hanging out at someone's house, or we would be hanging by the Webster Groves pool. When we were at each other's houses on evenings, weekends, and half days of school we would spend our time making out with our female partners. You know whoever was with who on any given day; we could never make up our minds about who we wanted to be with.

Out of all my friends, I distinguished myself above my peers when playing hockey.

While all my teammates played their regular team games and practices I manage to practice with one additional team. That team was the Webster Groves varsity hockey team. Since I got started with my projected high school team two years prior to me playing as a freshman it paved my way as being known as a top-notch player. Not to mention when all the freshman and sophomores I skated with became juniors and seniors as I was a freshman it put me up on their level above my current peers when they were freshman. Junior high is over and high school has begun.

Here is where my chaotic life as a high schooler commences. It's the summer before my freshman year, and I and my hockey buddies are playing on hand-picked teams for the summer. I'm still averaging more ice time than most of my peers with playing late night pickup games, or getting on "dead ice." So, it was all mine. Furthermore, since I knew all the ice rink staff and managers it was no problem for me to obtain that ice for free. My equipment was stored at the rink off and on in the varsity locker room. Not to mention that I am still dedicating time on dry land: running, working out, and practicing my shot on my Plexiglass at home. As you can see I am completely devoted to this sport while making myself the best of the best. Again, I am invited out for the AAA St. Louis Blues 82 team. My try-outs this year were outstanding and above all the other players. The coaches had noticed me. There are players that played on the team previous years, and the top ones usually get a pass while making the team automatically for the current year. During the try-outs, out of the new players trying to make the team I am the only one they noticed. I personally am pulled off the ice to speak with the head coach twice during try-outs. This is a good sign. The second time I am pulled I'm offered a contract. Here I am thinking this is my big break to get exposure while traveling. My biggest regret is turning that contact down.

Since playing on a traveling team is more expensive I had to get the approval of my father to make sure he can afford the bills, which he could at that time hands down. Money was no issue with my family for hockey expenses. I'm advised by my father to speak with the Varsity coach, Darrel before I accept the AAA contract. Side note: If a player plays on the AAA team he is banned from playing any junior varsity games due to the high skill level one needs to play at the AAA level. Darrel the varsity coach for Webster Groves talks me out of playing on the AAA team along with my father. At that time, I was okay with going back to my AA team, but I still had my reservations, because I would be missing out on much out of state exposure. I would be now playing on my AA team and the Varsity team or so I thought.

I still had to try-out for my varsity team and my AA team. I was a lock-in making the team since I had played on that team for many years now. All the high school guys knew me since I had already been skating with them for two years now. I had their respect as a player. When the varsity try-outs concluded, there is a list posted to see who was to play on what team, varsity or junior varsity. Like a gunshot to the head, I see that I am listed as a swing player. A swing player plays both on varsity and the junior varsity teams. I'm highly insulted by this, as I know my skill level is way above junior varsity, hints since I was skating with the varsity team for two years. Come to find out since I was only playing AA Darrel figured he could have me play both junior varsity and varsity to help out the junior varsity team win games. Get this, on the varsity team, I am starting on the first line with two other seniors as me a freshman with them. Why would a first line varsity player need to play on the junior varsity team? In addition, when I was given my team's jersey I was given the number 19. That was Jack's number as he graduated the year before I was a freshman. Darrel the coach planned to retire his number when Jack graduated; not allowing anybody else to wear that number, because he was such a talented player. Here I am now wearing that number for my high school team. Was that because my talent matched Jack's, or was I expected to exceed Jack's level of play? It only took a few games of me playing for the junior varsity before Darrel pulls me and only has me playing varsity. You probably can see a little narcissism in me during this time. With my top level of play, I am invited to try-out for the Select 15 team.

The Select 15 team is the best of the best fifteen-year old's in the tristate area all trying out for the same team. That is a lot of players. First, I tried out in St. Louis amongst all the top 15-year old's in my area. After that, only about 7 to 8 players from St. Louis are sent to Chicago for the final try-outs for this team. It turns out since I've distinguished myself as a real player it didn't matter what I did during the try-outs in St. Louis; I was already selected to go to Chicago. I didn't make the team that year, but they only took one kid from St. Louis, and his name was Ned. Ned's father played professional hockey in the NHL, so Ned was a shoe-in for the slot on the Select 15 team.

During my freshman and sophomore years of high school hockey, our team went to the state championships once my freshman year and we lost to Desmit high school. In my sophomore year, we lost out to CBC in the semi-finals. There were other opportunities to come.

I'm at home one summer afternoon and a man calls my father's apartment. He asks to speak to me saying it is in regard to hockey. I remember going to my father's wood colored brown desk and picking up that white telephone receiver. He tells me that he represents Robby Glanz Power Skating company. Robby Glanz is a power skating coach who teaches the L.A. Kings (professional hockey team) how to skate better and stronger during the regular season. During the summer, he travels with a group of strong players (usually older around 22-25) and teaches summer hockey camps. He offers me a job teaching at his camp in the St. Louis area. I gladly accept, plus I am paid to work. How did this man know my number?

Even though he offered me a job site unseen to only have heard about my own abilities; Robby hired me off the recommendation of a coach I have never heard off. When Robby called this coach, he asked for the top strong skater in St. Louis, and the coach instantly said my name. Turns out at the end of the camp I met the coach who recommended me. He had seen me play for years. Come to find out I was also teaching his own son how to improve his skating skill set. Hints why he recommended me because I was above all others. More work was to come. During that summer and the following one, I taught at the Breakaway hockey camp which was held at the Webster Groves Ice Rink. Now it was time to try-out for a much higher level of play.

The summer before my sophomore year I was invited to try out for the Junior B St. Louis Blues, again this team is a traveling team, and the age range goes up to twenty years old or so. I'm barely sixteen when I try out. While I was good enough to make the team the coach Jeff told me that I would have more exposure by trying out for an independent AAA team, the Affton Americans. The coaches were the Hendrix brothers, and they knew me well before I ever met them. I take that advice and show up for tryouts for the Affton Americans. Again, I have an amazing try-out, but that didn't matter, because I was already on the team when I showed up at the ice rink. I could have worn a tutu during try-outs and still made the team. Being on an independent AAA team meant that we still had to play our in-town games for our district, which we won every game hands down. We also traveled frequently to play other AAA teams, which we won most of those games as well. Since our team had an undefeated record in our district games we were automatically sent to regionals, which is a major tournament where the winner will then go onto nationals. The regional teams consist of the teams that win all or most of their districts games. That year at regionals we made it to the championship game against Naperville, but we lost. Still, these extra traveling games against AAA teams and regionals gave me great exposure for people to see my level of play, which is the right way to get an athletic scholarship to play college hockey. By the middle of my sophomore year of high school, my love for the sport begins to die.

I don't remember drinking much during my freshman year of high school, because I had a decent group of friends. I had my fellow teammates and the hockey cheerleaders who seemed to be very happy to be around me. I had one cheerleader who I was particularly fond of and her name was Jasmen. She had dark wavy hair and a face you could stare at for hours with her stunning beauty. I had no outside friends from the jock type people I hung around with except my Christian friends. During my freshman year, I was introduced to a youth group called Young Life. It is a group of teens who have given their lives to this so-called God person with Jesus as their savior. Here is where I meet Katy. Katy's older brother Billy originally introduced me to Young Life, which met on a weekly basis at Herold and Tiffany's house. They were an older adult couple who ran the Young Life group. Billy was two years ahead of me in high school, while Katy his younger sister who was one year ahead of me. One-week Billy explained to me that he would not be able to give me a ride to Young Life. He told me that his sister Katy would pick me up a 6:30 pm for the Christian group at my father's apartment. I told him that she should pick me up around back by the garages of the apartment my father and I lived in. I had reservations about being picked up by his sister, but he assured me that she was a good person and that she would make sure I would get home safely. Turns out Katy was a very special person who could walk into a room and light it up while bringing a smile to everyone in that room. She was a tall drink of water with long legs and brown shoulder length hair that appeared to be flowing down upon her shoulders. Her smile was something special. While her laughter was like the sounds of birds singing a song, just so naturally beautiful. I met Katy for the first time as I climbed into her parent's maroon Aerostar van. Apparently, Katy already knew who I was, and she could have picked me out of a group of fifty people or so. That night Katy had her friend with her, whose name was Jackie. When I said hello to both of them Jackie stated I had a sexy voice. It was a good way to break the ice as my anxiety levels were running high. Plus, getting a complimented about my sexy voice was always a good stroke to my ego. Just pointing out the narcissism here in me again. Even playing the elite levels of hockey that I played at, and my talent level played very high into my narcissism as well, such as making teams before I even started the try-outs for those teams.

During that next week at hockey practice, I mention to Billy that I thought his sister was fairly cute. As he replied that is not someone for me to date, because he knew what all high school boys are after, so I kept Katy on the friend level out of respect for Billy. Katy and I became good friends which was nice, and I'm very grateful to have ever known her. I had someone I could talk to about anything in this world or

whatever was on my mind. I always got the
feeling she liked me more than a friend
though, but I kept it at that, just friends out
of respect for Billy. What no one knew was
I figured eventually Katy and I could date
once in college as I matured more; she was
very mature for her age, so it was just me
who needed to grow up a bit.

Since Katy and I were friends I felt I had
hurt her feelings more than once as I dated
her friends knowing that I couldn't date her.
This I feel terrible about. I still had her in
mind in the long run for a real long-term
relationship down the line, but time
eventually ran out and the grim reaper took
her from me prematurely. Young life is
where Katy introduced me to Jeremy, who
became my best friend very fast.

I knew who Jeremy was long before
I met him. I never thought we would
become the best of friends. Jeremy had a
dark red four-door Saturn with two twelve-
inch sub-woofers in the trunk of his car. I
knew this because I saw him every morning
my freshman year when I was dropped off in
front of the school, and he would have his

stereo thumping while chain-smoking cigarettes in his car waiting for school to start. Tim was his friend, and he would be doing the same in his car, also while his massive stereo would be blaring. It was like they had these two parking spots in front of the school, and no one dares to park in those spots, which no one did. I thought at that time that we would not have much in common nor ever be friends, and it turns out a few months later we just clicked and became fast friends. Best friends.

Jeremy was a very unique person and one of a kind. His average dress was the wearing of black steel-toed combat boots, which had red laces. While wearing pants that were cut off just below the knees. He had short black cut hair that was cropped while his ears sported multiple earrings. He sported t-shirts that had different band logos on them. He also played guitar, and I was not musically inclined. At that time, I wore painter's pants and shoes of some sort, but I don't remember the type of shoes I wore back then. I also would sport a white cap that held college logos of where I would like to go for college and play hockey at. Jocks whore these white caps and were known as a "white cap." Our styles didn't match, and I figured on that alone we wouldn't click. I was wrong. I met Jeremy at a party on one special night.

Everybody was partying at Richard's house one night, and I was there, along with Katy. Jeremy was there too. I saw him across the crowded room and made some comment about him. Katy happened to be by me at that time in the corner as we were both not of the "cool" kid's status; we were just there at the party, and no one would have noticed if we weren't there either. She heard my comment about Jeremy, and she offered to introduce us. I declined as I had my preconceived notions that we wouldn't be a match to be friends. She responded that he was a nice guy and would love to make my acquaintance. She introduces us and things went well. I was surprised at how well we clicked, it is like our brains matched, and that was it; we became fast friends, which then became best friends. He taught me many things, such as not to judge people by stereotype, because often what is on the outside is not often what is on the inside. I use that knowledge on a daily basis when I find myself starting to judge people. Jeremy and I spent the rest of the year together side by side one without the other. It was as if we were one person. During the summer, Jeremy took me down to his parent's lake house at the Lake of the Ozarks. We bonded during that time making our friendship unbreakable.

The beginning of the end starts here. My life was perfect as I was playing top notch hockey, had a best friend, and life was good, or so I thought. As I was in Young Life, so was Jeremy. One-night Jeremy and I are running about in Webster causing much trouble but doing no harm literally. Jeremy is paged on his black Motorola pager. We find a pay phone. (Yes, a pay phone.) This is back in the late nineties, where people still used pay phones that were located on street corners. Jeremy returns the page, and we are given tragic news. The news was that Katy had been killed in a car accident. I myself didn't believe such news that night. She was currently working as a nanny that summer in Pennsylvania. We are told that Katy was driving to the market when a semi-truck jumped the median and hit them head-on. Jeremy and I rush over to the house where people are gathering to comfort one another. At this point, I would say I am in complete denial and shock. The rest of the night becomes a blur. The date is July 17th, 1998. I'll never forget that date again for the rest of my life. Katy's body is sent back to St. Louis for the funeral and burial.

I think it was a few days or so, but the wake was up next, then the funeral. Here is where I lost it and reality set in. I completely lost it. I cried uncontrollably. Luckily enough I had both Jeremy and Billy there to get me through Katy's passing. Even though Billy was Katy's older brother he held it together and was there for me to be a shoulder to cry on. Billy showed his remarkable character during this time, being a friend to me. I spent the entire wake crying and holding onto someone to deal with my grief.

I can remember being asked if I was ready to go up to Katy's casket. It was a very unreal moment for me. As I walked up towards Katy I could see her metallic light blue casket just like the innocence she possessed. She was only seventeen at the time. So, young and gone too soon. Katy had on a navy-blue blazer with a white blouse. Her body laid there peacefully, unable to more. I looked down at Katy, and I could see her body lying there, her soul was long gone. I became deeply saddened knowing that I would not ever see my dear friend again. Next, I had to face the funeral.

Katy was buried off of Big Bend Rd. I remember standing there watching the pastor man speak on behave of Katy as her coffin appeared to be levitating over the rectangle shape hole in the ground. It was as if I had stepped outside of my own body leaving just a zombie of a shell behind. As Katy's coffin was being put into the ground I found myself in frantic thought. I had to remember exactly where Katy's grave was and where this graveyard is located. It was a strange situation. As I explained what I was doing at the end of Katy's funeral luckily enough a friend named Mike who quickly pointed out some landmarks, so I would never forget where she was buried. I'm forever grateful to this friend, which has allowed me to visit Katy's grave many times over.

Besides being friends with Billy I was what I would consider close to Billy's and Katy's parents too. Katy's mom gave me her last school picture to keep with me sometime after Katy's passing. After nineteen years, I still have that same picture with me in my wallet. Never lost and never forgotten. When my troubles started after Katy's death I even stayed in Billy's house sleeping on the floor of their living room. They said I could stay in Katy's room, but I felt that would be too much for me.

The weeks to months after Katy's passing were a blur to me, but the deaths kept coming. Erica was killed by a drunk driver going the wrong way on the highway. She was Jim's older sister. I played hockey both in my youth with Jim and in high school. Then Brain fell off a mountain and was killed. Next, was Joe who they say drowned in the Meramec River, but many think he was murdered by a transient. All of these deaths hit our school very hard as they all happened in the summer of my freshman year as school was about to begin that September. Jeremy and I were there for each other to get through these tragic events that plagued the 98/99 school year. During those months, Jeremy and I were inseparable in bringing our brotherly bonds tighter together. It's an indescribable feeling knowing that you have another person in this world that meets you on the same brainwaves; one who is there for you know matter what. A person that stands by you in any time of need, without question. That was what Jeremy was to me, and I have never found anybody that comes close to what Jeremy and I were. There is more tragedy to come.

September 1st, 1998 was the first day of school, and that following day was the worst day of my life. During the first day of school, Jeremy and I had made plans to drive out to St. Peters about 30 to 40 minutes away from where we lived. We were going to pick up a van out there, so we could take a bunch of people out to a Christian rock concert that following weekend. I still had faith in God at this time. Things became garbled and we were supposed to go after school, but it wasn't till later that night that he called me to go, it was about 9 pm or so. I asked my father if I could still go and he said, "No." His thoughts were, it was the first day of school and tomorrow was the second. He figured it would be better to get a good night's rest instead of being out late at night. I hold resentments towards my father for this decision, because if I would have gone with him things could have turned out different. I apologized to Jeremy and tell him that we could go tomorrow after school. He said that he may still go tonight or tomorrow for sure. That was the last time I ever spoke to Jeremy, and it was on the phone, not even in person. He seemed fine when I told him I couldn't go, and I figured I would see him tomorrow at school.

The next morning came about. I would soon be given the worst possible news in the world and I was not expecting it. I'm almost ready to shove off to school as I want to get there early to find Jeremy sitting in his car smoking like any other day. The phone rings and it is Herold from Young Life. He asks me if I need a ride to school? I tell him my father is up and ready to take me, so I decline. Then Herold asks of me to wait there so he can drop by. At this time, I figure he might have gotten word that I was drinking some beers that past weekend, and he was going to rat me out. Again, I tell him that I was going to head to school, and I would drop by his house later after school let out. He begs me to wait until he arrives, so I give in and say, "Fine, I'll wait."

Herold arrives swiftly at my father's apartment. A knock at the doors comes about. Herold is not even through the door when he tells me. Jeremy died last night in a single-car crash. Fuck! I already knew what happened, and I don't believe it. My mind and body goes into shock, and I leave my body once again. All that is left is a shell of a zombie-like before. I'm told that I don't have to go to classes that day, but my zombie shell of itself says I can manage. Herold drives me to the school, while I don't remember bringing my book bag with me that awful day; I do remember bringing my bible for some reason. Even though shortly after this day my faith is broken, and it never healed or was restored back, like how it was before.

Herold drops me off, and I go to my first class. It was honors algebra. They announce Jeremy's death on the school's intercom. The announcer told students if being in class was too difficult for them that they could head down to some hallway where students were gathering to comfort each other. Jeremy's presence was so BIG over the school it is like the day stop since he was gone. Everybody in my class turns and looks at me as someone who was outed for being a thief. They know Jeremy and I were the best of buds, and they wanted to see what I was going to do. I sat in algebra class for a few minutes, maybe more. I was bewildered so I just got up and walked out, as a zombie from the walking dead. No one said anything to me.

I believe my intent was to go down to that hallway area, but I never made it. I walked the halls for god knows how long before I just sat down in one of the halls, to this day I do not remember what hall it was. I sat there next to someone's locker unknown to me while repeating this is not happening; it is not true. Why? During this time, Billy and Mike are frantically searching for me to make sure I am alright, and that I would not do something stupid. What that something was, who knows. Eventually, Billy and Mike find me babbling to myself in that hallway. I remember seeing them as they came running up to me. I'm unable to stand up and greet them in my sorrows. Billy pulls me up, and I fall back against those orange locker doors. They ask me many questions, but I am unable to answer them. I'm now mumbling random un-audible words and sentences. They decide to remove me from the school because they fear too many people would come up to me, which could cause me to lose it more. So, we left the school grounds.

I don't remember where we went that day, but I remember Billy and Mike being there for me. They allowed me to sit and be still. Meanwhile, I am mumbling, and I'm beside myself as each passing minute goes by; Jeremy's death hits me harder and harder. At the point, it was not like I could talk to them about how I was feeling, because I was outside myself, and all they would be doing was comforting a zombie imposture of myself. Jeremy's death hit me like a Mac truck speeding down a highway at ninety miles per hour, just like the truck that crashed into Katy on that awful day.

I knew Jeremy took pills for some mental health reasons, but during our friendship, I only knew about parts of Jeremy's own troubles. He was a manic depressive (before they started calling it Bi-Polar disorder). Jeremy had also attempted suicide the year before we meet. He had slashed open his left wrist at a party at Richard's house. Making two long wounds across that wrist, which after the wound was closed and the stitches healed the wound looked like an equal (=) sign. Jeremy's was a "cutter" also. This would be something we would grow to have in common shortly after his passing.

When Jeremy found out that I started cutting myself shortly after Katy's death he became livid with me and did not want me to end up with a "cheese grater" of an arm like his was. Katy's death is what sparked my first "cutting" episode, which followed by many more after Jeremy's passing.

On the night of Jeremy's wake, I don't remember how I got there or how I got home it was very surreal. Due to the major damage of the car crash, Jeremy's parents had a closed casket. I feel this is one thing that prevented me from getting closure after Jeremy's funeral, not being able to see him one last time and say my goodbyes. His coffin was jet black, and it shined like it was given a wax job meant for a Lamborghini. There was an immense amount of students and people who showed up for Jeremy's wake. He may not have lived long, but he had touched a lot of people in his short life, including me.

I remember walking into the place, and I saw the gigantic line of people waiting to go by the casket and pay their respects to Jeremy's parents. I did not stand in line. I was standing about the halfway point of the line in utter shock that this event was true. I am devastated and lost during this tragic night. After some time standing there, Billy asked me if I was ready to go up to the casket, and I said yes. I didn't get inline either; Billy walked me right up to the front of the line, and I just stared blankly at the casket. No one bothered to tell me that I had to get in line to say goodbye to my dear friend. I spoke briefly to Jeremy's parents, and I told them I was sorry for their loss as Jeremy's was a dear friend of mine, which they knew. I would mourn his loss forever along with Katy's too.

I couldn't tell you how long I was at his wake because I felt outside of myself without any awareness. Later, a few weeks down the road I heard a story that someone gave a Zippo to Jeremy's parents telling them it was his favorite. Jeremy's father opened the casket slightly and slid the lighter in. The person who gave the Zippo to Jeremy's parents said that he could see his shoes when the casket was opened ever so slightly. I'm told that Jeremy's parents had him buried with his black combat boats as he would have wanted that.

After the funeral ended everybody left the church and headed to the graveyard. There where so many people there that the line of cars covered the entire road through the graveyard from where Jeremy would be buried, which was close to the exit of the graveyard all the way back to the entrance. Jeremy had much of an impact on people he had met, and he had touched their lives greatly, along with my life too.

I'm so numb during the talk given by the pastor guy hearing that Jeremy is no longer with us and how he has gone to a better place in God's heaven. At the end, people sang Amazing Grace and then begin to leave. I watch intensely as they lower Jeremy's coffin into the ground. I was standing by the road in the cemetery next to this big tree and a randomly placed trash can. The trash can is still there to this day. Some time goes by and Billy comes up to me and says that they are about to start throwing dirt down to fill in the grave. He wants to know if I wanted to watch this as it might be very painful for me or should we go? I tell him I wanted to watch because I felt that Jeremy could still come back to life and open his jet-black coffin while he climbs out of the hole in the ground. His grave is now filled in, and we leave.

As we are heading to the car Mike quickly points out landmarks again, so I may find and revisit Jeremy's grave. That is something I do many times over. Billy thinks it might be a good idea to just get away from all the people, and we head out to a park where it will be quiet and still. We go to a secluded park where our minds can process the events surrounding and leading up to Jeremy's death/suicide.

Jeremy was driving on a darkened highway as he was getting onto the exit ramp. The police said he most likely fell asleep behind the wheel and crashed into a solid dense cement poll; the ones that hold up highway bridges and such. This is a lie. Unfortunately, Jeremy intentionally crashed his car while driving at high speeds into that poll. Jeremy for one likes to speed, but no one gets off of the highway and onto the exit ramp doing 100 mph and falls asleep. I know this because later I did much speeding in my day, and while doing 100 mph one would have to be holding the steering wheel with both hands while focusing on controlling the car. You don't just fall asleep while doing that. After all of this I'm still troubled by the fact that I was supposed to be with him that night, and if I was with him things could have turned out different. I was supposed to be with Jeremy that night in the car. Not being there has greatly affected me, while even haunting me for years and years.

About a week or so after the funeral Billy asks me if I would like to go to the crash site and look around. He thinks this could help give me closure in Jeremy's passing. So, we go. When we get there, I don't feel like this is the spot Jeremy crashed at, but then again, I have been numb with grief since his passing. As I am looking at all the debris I notice a utility knife laying there. It was a knife Jeremy was given about a month before he died. I picked up the shining duel handle knife and realize that this belongs to him. I'm grief is stricken with heartache.

My sophomore year starts off like shit. My fellow hockey players, mainly Billy see that I am struggling with both Katy's and Jeremy's deaths. So, Billy and Mike have my locker moved from the sophomore hallway in the senior hallway. That way I am around them more, and if I ever needed anything they could help me out. Maybe a month goes by that first semester before I start having major trouble. As I continued to get A's in my classes, and my playing on the ice is outstanding people think I'm doing okay, but I'm not on the inside. One teacher did notice my pain.

I don't remember this teacher's name and at the current time of this writing, I am deeply saddened that I have no way how to contact her now at the present time. Since the writing of this book, I found her on Facebook, but I never got a response. She was my social studies type teacher; I think the class was called Continence and Cultures. This teacher's kindness towards me in the middle of my turmoil greatly affected me, and I'll never forget her because of it. During classwork time, I would often go up to her desk to talk or ask her questions about life. She also explained how to "hug" a candle, so it burns evenly. I noticed this really cool looking wood pen and pencil set that sits in a wooden case that opens and closes like a clamshell does. I tell her I would like to have it and she says, "No." So, after much negotiation, I make a bet with her.

Since I already had an A in her class for the first semester of school, and I often skipped her class and others as well she was concerned that my A could drop. I bet her that if I get an A for the second semester that she would have to give up the pen and pencil set. She accepts my bet. She also tells me that I can come to her class anytime, any day if I needed to sit somewhere and be still. Turns out due to my turmoil I wouldn't be around for that second semester, because of my drug and alcohol addiction that would be forming.

The second semester is over, and I am running rampant around town slowly destroying myself. I was on a self-destructive path, which didn't matter to me. I knew it was summer time as people who I was in school with were now home during the days. It might have been a week or two since I am not completely sure because I was high on pot all day every day at this time. I'm home one day during this time, and I'm most likely getting stoned by myself when the mail comes. I have a package. I don't remember if there was a return address on the package or not. I rip open the light brown envelope with gusto to find a note and the wooden pen and pencil set from my special teacher. I'm deeply moved by this gesture even though I am high as a kite on that day. I don't remember what the note said due to my marijuana use at that time. This pen and pencil set has traveled with me through thick and thin. I have kept it safe, and I still have it to this very day some 19 years later. Currently, I use the pen to write daily entries in my journal and for my planner dates. After Jeremy's death, it all starts to go downhill from here like a bullet train heading straight to hell and making no stops on the way to get off at. Drugs and alcohol really got a hold on me with a grip so tight that one would need the jaws of life to break me free. I become a full blow addict within months after Jeremy's death. Nor did I care what could happen to me and my life.

Drugs & Alcohol
Part I

Chapter 5: The Teen Therapy Years

I was put into therapy by my parents after my dear friends have passed. They were told by the other parents that it might help me if I talked to someone about my problems. No one explained to me what I was doing in therapy. This lead to much confusion for me on why I was there in the first place.

So one day my mom grabs me and says we are headed out. I go along with her not knowing where we were going. Turns out we were going to the therapist office. I wasn't happy about it once I got there. Who wants to talk about their problems anyway. Also, why bother someone else with your problems, right?. Ever notice if you break the therapist apart it becomes, "The Rapist." Just a thought. It's someone's job to mind rape you in the long run.

What was therapy supposed to do for me? I tell some guy my friends are dead and he can make it all better. I didn't understand why I was there, nor did my family explain to me how some unknown person to me can help me with my problems. I was at a loss from the start.

Here I am this angry little teenager sitting in some hotshot's office with his fancy degrees hanging on the wall and what not. One, I'm pissed because I'm there and I don't know why. No one, not even the therapist explains what I'm doing there.

The nerve of the first therapist who asks me what is going on with me. I tell him nothing. I treat this first encounter like a police interrogation. I tell him nothing, deny everything, and admit nothing. Fuck him!

I make it through like three visits with this guy and he refers me off to a college. It was more like here this kid is impossible you deal with him. Don't think I noticed this either. And it happened quite a few more times. I went through a handful of therapists before my parents gave up on the concept, but it was more like everybody gave up on me.

So, my parents hauled me off to another therapist, "The Rapist." This one asks me more questions, but I treat him like shit. One thing I do this is because I never trusted men in my life. My parents should have gone with a woman. Here is where I start to play mind games with this therapist. Telling him I hear voices and shit, people are after me and what not.

Eventually, that guy refers me to another college. I'm starting to see a pattern here. It's like here this kid is fucking impossible here you take em. Finally, my parents get fed up and stop sending me to therapy when I show up for an appointment I had forgotten about, but before the appointment, I had spent about three hours smoking weed. I was not ready to talk to some head doctor in this present state. My parents demanded I come.

I show up stoned out of my mind. This is the first time I had met this therapist. He began by asking me questions about my life. I have no clue what this person is asking me as I'm completely stone. I have trouble forming answers that would be of a serious nature without laughing. He becomes angry in nature. I point out that he has trouble with anger issues and should look into it. That pisses him off more.

Eventually, he called my parents into the room and explained to them that he has better things to do with his time. I don't even think he bothers to give them another therapist number to pass me off to, I was officially a lost cause. No one wanted to work with me, but I can see why due to my behaviors I demonstrated.

In my late teens I was put back into therapy, but this time I was willing. Moreover, I had a female therapist. I was able to grow and feel comfortable talking with this female therapist. But that all changed one day.

I was living with my father at this time and I had no car. He was driving me to

145

my weekly appointments, with the female therapist. Then blam he blows up and starts to yell at me. Complaining that I am wasting my time with this therapist and such. I'm caught off guard by this explosion of words. So, I quickly come up with the idea of joining the Army and that is how that came about. I joined the Army on a whim, one quick thought to calm my father down from his tirade of verbal abuse on me.

At my therapy appointment, I discuss this option with my therapist and she cautions me to make sure it will be okay for me to join with my mental disorders and medications.

My very last therapist during these years I felt that she was doing me much good, but due to my father's anger, our therapy ended prematurely. During our sessions, I felt that I could really open up to her and start to work out my problems. Is there regret that I didn't finish therapy with her and joined the Army. If I hadn't come up with the Army idea and finished my therapy would my life had turned out different?

I took her word with a grain of salt. But when it all came down to it I went off my meds once again and joined the Army on a whim or an impulse. My whole life seemed to be a matter of impulsive decisions.

Chapter 6: The Dreaded Teenage years

This is the beginning of the end of my life. My downfall has commenced; I was choosing to take a self-destructive path without ever knowing that that was the choice I was making. Alcohol and drugs will do that to people. It did it to me, and addiction doesn't discriminate either. At this point in my life I'm sixteen completely clueless about life but think I know all, and I'm pissed off at this God person I gave my life up for because he took the most important people in my life away. I was torn apart by Katy's and Jeremy's deaths. I had no clue how to cope with these tragic events in my life, nor was I open to other people's advice. They had no idea what I was going through. They couldn't walk in my shoes. I found beer again at this time in my life, and I began to use it as a coping tool. It worked well.

Even though I had drunk beer prior to this I had never gotten drunk off it before. I was attending a party one night and got ahold of some beer from one of the guys there. I don't remember the brand, but I knew if I drank enough of it, I'd get drunk. That was my goal that night. As I was drinking the beer I noticed that the alcohol numbed my pain. What a feeling! It was an amazing thing to consume this liquid, and the pain stopped. Here I go off to the races.

I was also the type of kid to do things, "Big". There is a saying, "Go big or go home." "Anaheim or bust," was the saying my AAA hockey team used when we were competing to go to nationals. Anaheim was the town that where nationals were held that year. Now for me, it was with booze and drugs.

It is the Thursday before the weekend, and I begin to seek out how I can posse many beers. I find a senior classmate I heard had a fake ID, and I tell him he is going to buy me beer. I tell him I have cash and looked into his eyes with a stare that could burn through wood. This senior is aware of my current turmoil, and he caves in and asks me what brand of six-pack would I like. I say, "No, twelve pack." Go big or go, home right? He buys me the booze while I waited outside. After I get my beer I store it for the night, but not without drinking three beers first. I figure this way I could sleep and not be tormented by my devastating loss. I was in pain and this was the only thing that could kill my pain.

It's Friday night, and I retrieve my beer from my backpack of course, who would look there right? I find a party one I'm most likely not welcomed at, but I crash it anyway. I need a spot to drink my wonderful new medication. At this party, I discover an additional medication.
I'm drinking my beer to kill my pain in one of the bedrooms in the house since I wasn't

feeling that sociable. A group of guys comes in, and they intended on smoking some pot amongst themselves. I handed a beer to one of the guys and joined in. I begin smoking the pot as it gets passed around. I feel the effects as the joint makes its way around the circle. Man, this feeling was even better than the beer. When the pot hits me I realized that I no longer have a care in the world. I'm completely numb all over. I no longer posse emotions of sadness and pain. All I can do is smile and laugh as I tilt my head back, not having a care in the world. Any problem from now on will fall off my body like water cascading down a waterfall. Before the party ends I decide I must have some of this wonderful herb.

I approach my fellow classmate who had the biggest bag of pot. I tell him I would like to buy what he has left on him. He declines to sell the pot to me. This is another person who is aware of my loss, and I tell him again that I would like to purchase any amount he can part with. So, he says he can part with thirty dollars' worth, which is about six grams. I buy it up quickly. Within a couple of hours, I am stoned and drunk, but I make my way home. I think?

During this period, I was living with my father in his apartment about two miles from school. Since I don't want to get caught with the pot by my father; I decided to hide it in the storage space which is in the garage of his apartment. I've drunk all my beer so there is no need to load my backpack up. I'm already thinking about how I can obtain more beer for Saturday. The addiction is beginning to form. During this time beer and weed really make me feel numb to normal, so I sought out more.

I wake up Saturday morning, and my father goes off to play tennis for a few hours. I'm already back in my sorrow and self-loathing. I remember the pot that I have. I run down our stairwell as I round the corner to the storage area while using my hand to hold the ninety-degree turn. I snatch the bag of green pot out from behind the two by four as it rested on the crossbeam. I rushed back to the apartment and dump my dope out onto one of my textbooks. Then, "Fuck." How am I going to smoke this is the first thought that crosses my mind as the pot hits the book. So, I phone a friend.

I called a friend of mine who I know smokes pot. As the phone is ringing and ringing I am glad once my friend picks up. I explained to him my dilemma. He quickly becomes the MacGyver smoker over the phone. My friends explained to me how to make a "foil pipe." I thank him and slam down the phone. Off to the kitchen, I go. After I have torn my proper piece of foil off I use my black Bic pen making the foil into a tube. Then I slide the pen from the foil ever so smoothly. My next move is flipping my pen over, and I use the cap end to bend up a small portion of the aluminum tube. Now I have my smoking device, but where to smoke?

At sixteen with an abusive father, I'm smart enough not to smoke at his place. So, off I go walking to the park as I feel this would be the best place to smoke in peace to kill my pain. While walking to the park I'm already in the addict type of mine only thinking about my drugs, and how I can't wait to inhale them. After a few miles of walking, I arrived at this beautiful green grass filled park. I find this spot that is right on the edge of the park's boundaries, which is edged by a wooded area. I sit down and smoke my drugs. As I inhale the pot smoke a warmth comes over me. When the pot takes hold, I have once again lost all my pain and sorrow. This feeling is just what the doctor ordered; there's no more sadness, anger, self-loathing, and grief. I fell in love with Mary Jane; a cure-all to my problems, since I am unable to cope with Katy's and Jeremy's deaths. Not to mention the fact that I did not have any healthy coping skills in my tool bag to use like I do now. Nor was I ever taught any beforehand. Thanks, Mom and Dad.

As time went by during this period after Jeremy's and Katy's death I turned down any help that was offered to me that would be a healthy way for me to handle their deaths, such as talking about it. This is where I started to push the good people in my life away, and after more trying on their part I was still cold to them and away they went. They even pleaded with me and offered to help in any possible, which fell on deaf ears on my part. I didn't even realize during this time I was losing some of the most important people in my life, like Billy. I kept turning to drugs and alcohol at this point, because that way they numbed everything all over for me which seemed to be the right choice, turns out it wasn't. No one wakes up one day and says, "I wish I would be a drug addict." No one asks to be an addict, but if someone is in enough pain before they know it drugs and alcohol grabs ahold of them pulling them down and for me, I had no clue it was happening at that time. I was completely blind to how my forming addictions took friends from me, affected my class grades, school attendance, and most importantly had torn my desire and love to play hockey.

My sophomore year was full of its ups and downs like riding a roller-coaster with nobody at the controls. I was going through manic and depressive episodes rapidly in my constant shifting of moods. My decent friends were slowly disappeared from my life like a person does when they walk into the woods in a heavy fog until they've vanished like a magician on stage. Those friends were quickly replaced by my "drug" friends. Those guys had no problem stealing from me, screwing me over, and abandoning me in random places. It was not all a one-way street though as I did the same to them. When addicts are together the only thing that matters to them is getting high or drunk, even both would be the ultimate answer. The only goal of an addict relationship is to find drugs and alcohol and nothing else. We don't truly care about one another, just the drugs. These remedies are the cure to my depression. No one understands what was going on with me at this time, while the people who cared about me watch myself self-destruct.

My problems had grown huge like the State Puff Marshmallow Man. I couldn't realize the help that was offered as I chose to put these people off. It hurt, but not till a later time in my life when I realized I had lost all of these good people in my life.

As months follow Jeremy's and Katy's deaths people noticed that I often appeared depressed. My depression follows me around like a dark black cloud raining directly over my head. It was the start of the darkness to come into my life. I often expressed anger and irritation towards others as the hard rain rained down on me. I became short and aggressive with my teachers that semester after Jeremy had passed. I even threatened my Latin teacher with harm.

One day I'm sitting in Latin class angrier than usual, especially at that God person that took my dear friends away from me on those tragic days. I'm currently sober now, but my focus is thinking about when the next time I can get drunk and high again. So, I decided to take a nap on that light brown desk that is attached to my cheap plastic chair. My Latin teacher decides to wake me up with a question that I deem stupid and trivial.

I expressed to her that I was sleeping and waking me up was a bad idea. She demands that I answer the question and that I do it in Latin. This just angers me more since we rarely ever answer our questions in

Latin. I answered it and get it right, but I expressed my frustration to her about her bothering me with such a trivial and pointless question. I currently have an A in her class. Furthermore, I explained to her in detail how I could harm her for retribution. At first, she laughs it off as just a comment. Then I tell her I could come to her house and cause her much harm, which could have been laughed off too but, I decide to rattle off her home address as well. It's always a bad idea to call my bluff because I rarely bluff in life.

I believe my graduating class was the last class where one (I) could threaten a teacher and somewhat mean it without being instantly expelled, but Columbine ruined that. My parents were notified of this incident. When questioned by my parents and guidance consular about this event I respond in a similar manner, and I tell them to "Fuck Off, I'm angry at everybody." I was asked to switch Latin classes. My depression at this point was already in the gutter, and the actions that I did were of no factor to me while considering their consequences. Nothing anymore mattered in my life except one thing, playing hockey.

The drugs and alcohol are the only tools I use to self-medicate, but I was able to pull it together for hockey practices and games. During this time, I'm playing on two teams, where one is a highly prestigious team. My hockey teams manage to take up a lot of my time. The downfall is when the drugs start to fight against my time playing hockey. High or not on the ice I was still gold, my level of play was top notch.

Since I am sixteen and able to drive, my mother finds a car for me to purchase so I can get to my games and practices easily. It is an eighty-something piece of shit Buick. The color is a reddish brown, four-door, with steel front and back bumpers on it. The thing is a tank. Its costs are one thousand dollars. I have the cash to buy it outright since I was quite the little saver when I was a tiny kid, not to mention all the cash I saved from my earnings while teaching hockey camps, referring, and doing the clock/scoreboard for other hockey games. Plus, my lawn business as well. My parents never realized how this car would be my ultimate ticket to scoring drugs and alcohol with my new-found freedom.

My car gave me an easy spot to hide my pot and booze. Moreover, it allowed me to get high/drunk on my way home from practices and games. Living with my father I might have been caught, but when practices/games end late into the night, and I have school the next day it is easy to come home and go straight to bed, thus allowing me to lay in bed as my troubles slide off me as water moves smoothly down as on a waxed car.

Jeremy's dad Greg calls me one day out of the blue. I decided to meet him for lunch. We chat a bit about Jeremy and life. He asks if I have time to follow him back to his house. Greg gives me Jeremy's two twelve-inch, "Kicker" subwoofers. I'm honored by the thoughtful gift and am very touched. While dealing with everything in my life: the deaths of my friends, hockey, drugs, alcohol, and current friends. My first suicide attempt comes about. Depression overwhelmed me during this period, such as a title wave that comes crashing down on me engulfing me with melancholy. I missed my friends dearly. I didn't know what to do with my life, and I felt as if things were slowly falling apart. I formed a plan to kill myself. I pick the time, date, and place. This leaves me in complete control while the things in my life are completely out of control. All that is left is to write my first suicide note, and this wouldn't be my last. I complete the note, and I start to feel better because the end is near, my pain will soon be gone forever.

While writing the note my thoughts are I want to covey my death is no one's fault, besides my anger at this so-called God person. I wanted my letter to say a proper goodbye to my friends who meant the most to me because I never got my goodbyes with my dear departed friends.

Unfortunately, my mother finds this note in the outfit that I planned to wear when I will do the deed. What a blessing this will be. They tricked me into seeing a consular at the hospital. I speak to the doctor guy and tell him I'm fine. Nothing is wrong with me. The doctor swiftly pulls out my suicide note that my parents have given him. I explain to him that it was just an expression of my pain and that I had no desire to carry it out. I wasn't the top-notch liar that I'm today, and he doesn't buy it. He begins talking about the possibility of me staying at the hospital for a few days. I reject this idea.

I reject this idea because for one I have better things to do. Plus, I didn't feel I had anything wrong with me mentally. I just wanted to die and see my dear friends again. My pain was too much and living day to day has become unbearable. I wanted to leave Earth so to speak and move on. This was the way I thought would be the best way to do it. Ending my life.

Now, I'm pissed off and have a desire to go back home. I begin to yell at the doctor while calling him an idiot and so forth. I hear the door open behind me. I spin around like a top because I sense danger is near. Yep, I'm right. There are these two gigantic men standing there in white coats. Yes, they still wore white coats back then. They attempted to take me away, but I don't go without a fight. Eventually, they overpower me two against one. Not a fair fight if you ask me.

I'm in a psych ward for the first time in my life, and not the last either. My days are filled with juice and groups, while my other free time is spent talking to nurses and psychiatrists. I'm disgruntled during this time dealing with the medical professionals. I'm put on medications, but I don't remember which ones they were back then. There are other times I agree to a stay in the psych ward, but within hours of getting there, I'm ready to leave. I then begin my verbal manipulation to the staff and doctors telling them what they want to hear, in order for me to be discharged promptly. Those people never care anyway. I'm discharged about a week later, and I go back to school.

It only takes me about a week to get back into my old routines of drugs and alcohol. Furthermore, I stop taking the pills the doctors had prescribed me a week ago. I would have stayed on them if someone had taken the time to explain to me what they were and why I needed them. My only new symptom is that now I've started to skip my classes to ingest drugs and alcohol.

Now, I am dating a nice young lady named Kelly. We've only been dating a couple of weeks. Kelly has light red hair with pale white porcelain skin and was of average height. Her lips were always in a pouty form, but it was sexy as hell. She had a face that would just make me smile while having the honor to look at her. I found her gorgeous; she was a goddess from heaven.

I and my friend Richard decided to wake up early before school one day so we could smoke pot and get high. This would be a day of tragedy to come, and I never saw it coming. Richard and I are very stoned, and we head off to school. When we arrived at school we go inside and head to the sophomore hallway. We talk amongst the sophomores (our current class), and then we see a vice principal/guidance consular coming our way. We burn out of our group and head to the senior hallway. Again, this guy shows up, and we become paranoid and decided to leave once again. While pot effects how you think, and feel it can make you paranoid, so we decided to go talk to the freshman. Kelly is a freshman. We chat them up a bit, and at first, I don't notice that Kelly is not there. Furthermore, the principal shows up in the freshman hallway. Richard and I now come overly paranoid and decided to leave school for the day all together. The dam guy kept following us around. Marijuana causes paranoia.

To sum it up we get high before school and become so paranoid at school that we think the principal knows that we are high, so we ditch school altogether. Why did we even bother to wake up early? Our first stop is to get high again in the park. We do that and drop by my mother's house to smoke more pot since she was at work. Then it comes to me. Kelly was not at school this morning.

I figure that she must be at home, and if her parents are at work we could hang out there for the rest of the day. I phone Kelly. Her father answers the home phone, and I ask to speak to her. He says that she is not home, and I hang up while being stoned and all. After I hang up I realize that if she is not at home, nor school she should be somewhere. I called back. Again, I get her father, and I explain the dilemma of Kelly not being at school nor at home. So, I ask, where is she? His response is none of your business and hangs up. I become confused, and I called back once again. I explain that I am her boyfriend and am worried about her. Once again, I get a negative answer, and I hang up.

I say to Richard that this is some real BS. So, we smoke some more pot. While smoking, I become enraged with her parents, so I call back once again, but this time I threaten them with harm if they don't tell me where she is. The next call I tell them I know where they live, and I could mess them up big time. Over the course of the next few calls, I'm smoking more and more pot and making threatening calls. It gets to the point where I tell them that I'm going to come to their house and kill myself. I explain it will be like Romeo and Juliet. I call back one more time as this has become fun for me now threatening them with anything I can think of. This time a police officer identifies himself and says that the calls must stop otherwise there would be charges to face. I tell him to, "Fuck Off," and hang up. Remember when my drug habit built to an addiction I lost all respect for authority figures, especially cops. Now I'm pissed and it's time to go to Kelly's parents' house while making them face the music. Richard and I leave my mother's house, and we are off to the races.

When we are about half way there Richard asks me if I'm really going over there. I say yes and he wants to bail. I must turn my Buick around and drop him off at his house. I do that, and I'm flying back the way I came, back to Kelly's house. I should mention while driving to her house that I have my bag of dope and a handful of butterfly knives. One could see that I'm not very stable at this point, but I've already set off for the races, while not caring what could happen to me. Go Big or Go Home, right?

My red Buick comes to a skidding halt in front of Kelly's parents' house. I'm not sure what to do now, so I sit in my car while the stereo plays Kaci & JoJo's, "All My Life." The weather has turned to rain at this point of the day. The day started off sunny and cloudless. The weather seemed to change with my mood dark and dreary. The time is about 2 pm. After a couple of minutes, I look in my review and out of my windshield and see cop cars flying in from both sides. I figure I better do something, or I could be in big trouble. So, I slit both of my wrists (the wrong way this time), but the blood flows out of my wrists in torrents as the wounds spread open like the Grand Canyon. As the cop approaches my car he says to open up. I respond be holding up my bleeding wrist. He says open the door or the window will be broken. I open the door and step out, wrists bleeding and all. He tells me to keep my hands up while he searches me, which I comply. My knives fell off my lap as I was getting out of my car while seeing that I kicked them underneath my car. The cop clears me and then begins to wrap my wrists in gauze while I wait for the ambulance.

During this episode, I slit my wrists to one, prove a point that I would, and two, I didn't want to go to jail, so I figured the injured wrists would at least get me to the hospital before jail, and hopefully, I could work it out from there. In my mindset, I always feel things can always be worked out after the fact. In the same note, I could have cared less if the cop lets me bleed out and die because then my misery would then be over.

Instead, my sentence would be a two-week stay in the psych ward, again and some stitches. The police and Kelly's parents never bothered to file any charges against me. I guess they figured out that I had enough problems to work on instead. I did find out where Kelly was in the next day or so. Turns out she was on some psychiatric medication and the night before she had tried to kill herself by taking a bunch of those pills. Psychologically speaking I guess we were made for each other. Moreover, I was right about my Romeo and Juliet scenario. Go figure huh?

We both get discharged from the hospitals. Of course, we stayed at separate hospitals, I was at St. Anthony's, and she was at St. Johns. I spend a few days at home before I go back to attend my classes at Webster. Kelly went to Webster high also, but when she was discharged she did not go back there. Eventually, I found out she was put in some group home or something of that nature. We did exchange letters through mutual friends when we could.

When I went back to school my parents encouraged me to find some of my "Good" friends that I used to spend time with. I do this. I get together with a buddy of mine that I played varsity hockey with at Webster, his name was Charles. He was a second line player for the team, while I was a first line player, which meant I was much better than he was at the sport. While knowing that all the jocks at our school drank I offered up the idea of getting some vodka for the party after the game on Friday. He was only a year older than me, so he could not be the one that purchases the vodka. Charles gets the idea to ask Andy to get the vodka for us. Andy graduated the year before I started high school, but I knew him since I was skating with the team two years before my freshman year. Andy does not pay for the booze, but he still obtains it though. This guy is like almost seven feet tall. We tell Andy that we want vodka, so how he steals the liquor is that he walks down the aisle next to the liquor aisle and reaches over the top shelve around the area of the booze we want. Then he sticks the bottle down his pants and walks out.

Andy gives us the bottle and says ten dollars, please. We pay Andy and leave. I think it is a Wednesday or Thursday at that time. That is a long way from Friday. Charles and I both agree, so we go to his mom's house to drink a little bit. I'm sure this is not what my parents had in mind when they ask me to find some good friends. Huh? We drink a little bit and save the rest for Friday night.

Our game ends and we win on Friday. All the hockey players shower up and head to Charles's house to party.

Charles and I share the vodka bottle during the party, but I get word of a better party going on, and I want to leave. After Charles and I argue for a minute or two about the vodka, and who's owned it. We decided that my share would be poured into an old two-liter soda bottle, then off I went. Of course, I don't remember where I went, or how I got home that night, but I did drink all my vodka, which was just under a half of a bottle.

It is not even weeks before I get back into my old ways of using drugs and drinking while hanging out with the start of what my drug family will become. These guys and girls are great; all of them knew how to get any kind of drug one could think up. We all slept with each other like people trading baseball cards. We are at a party one night and the cocaine guy shows up.

The cocaine guy is called to a party that I was attending to sell some coke to a couple of people. This dude is awesome. As he is walking through the house he grabs the two people who called him to score some cocaine. They all go into the bathroom and shut the door, but I managed to slide through the crack as the door is closing. I can sniff out drugs at a party better than the drug-sniffing dogs' cops use.

We are all in the bathroom now. Me, the cocaine guy, and the two prospective buyers. He offers a bump (a line of cocaine) to all of us. I gladly snort mine right up, like a Hoover vacuum cleaner. I don't feel much at first. The coke man bags up what he sells to the other guys. He then tells them to send in two girls. They leave. He offers me another bump. I gladly accept his offer. The girls come in and we all do a line. This goes on for half an hour or thereabouts, but I never leave the bathroom. He finally asks me if I planned on buying any coke. I just tell him that I'm here just to do cocaine. He seems to be okay with that, and we do two more lines. Hours pass and the night goes on. I'm still with the cocaine guy, and it is about 3 am. I guess it's a bad sign when you're with someone you don't know, and now we are in an unknown house, but the only reason I'm still with the guy is for the free cocaine. I'm told I ended up doing about a gram of coke that night, which is a lot unless your George Jung, especially when it's my first time ever doing coke, but not my last. In case you don't know who, George Jung is they made a movie about him called, "Blow" and he is played by Johnny Depp.

Time passes on and I'm still doing drugs and drinking almost daily now. I've met a new friend, who is named Justin. Again, I was somewhat aware of Justin, but I have never met him before. Justin and I become great friends after our first encounter, but he is no Jeremy.

I'm at home one afternoon, getting high as usual, and my friend Elaine called me and says Justin is over at her house harassing her, and that my girlfriend (at that time) Elle was with him. I go flying over there in a rage for some reason. I guess the phone call got me all worked up. By the time, I get there I see Elle and Justin, while Elaine flies out into the street and jumps into my car. She says just to drive, so I headed back to my house. Justin and Elle follow, like cops in hot pursuit. When I get there, I jump out of my car and pull a knife. I tended to carry lots of knives with me during this period of my life. They came in very handy. I run out into the street and Elle's car comes to a skidding halt, but Justin was driving. I yell at Justin, "Wanna go? Let's go!" Then I preceded to slash my right arm with my knife since I'm left-handed. Then blood comes rushing out like people running out of a burning building. Justin jumps out of the car and says he doesn't want to fight. As this episode wines, down, Justin and I become friends.

Justin was a beer drinker as I was too. Any substance would do as long as it messed me up. During this time of my life I used substances to numb myself from the reality I lived it. It was too painful to tackle sober. The drugs and alcohol gave me an outlet to release my pain so I could function during my day. This made perfect practice for my adult self in my twenties.

Basically, Justin always found beer for us to drink, and I got the pot and other drugs. We partied at my mother's house a lot during this time because my mother was never home as she was always staying with her current boyfriend.

I'm having another alcohol and drug-fueled party at my mother's house. My friend Richard and I are being the hosts of this party. We get about half-way through the party and Richard informs me that we are down to our last ten beers of the thirty pack. So, I say screw it let's go get more, but we take what's left of our beer with us. Richard and I hop into my Buick and head to the liquor store, but on the way, we are halted by two cops. They claim they say Richard drank from a can, but Richard and I are completely smashed at this point anyhow. Moreover, the cops find bats and other weapons on us. As they searched us without probable cause, but cops do that all the time. I think we are totally fucked at this point. Long story short they let us go and say to head back home. Isn't it great when the cops know you are trashed and are nice enough to say drive drunk home? Upon our arrival home, we find the party going strong, but my mother has arrived home. For some reason, she is okay with the party, but I'm beside myself with what happened with the cops, and them taking what was left of our beer. As I am standing there in her living room, now updated to nineties style I darted for the kitchen and grab the trusty steak knife. I then preceded to slash at my right arm until blood is free-flowing from all cuts. I can't tell you why I cut myself at that moment, but I had the impulse and needed something else to relieve my current stress level. The level increased when I saw my mom partying without guests. Don't ask me why, but that is when I lost it!

It has been about a year since I have seen Kelly. One-night Justin and I are partying, and I am handed the phone to my mother's house. It's Kelly. She was given a furlough from her special home for the weekend, and her parents allowed her to go out with some friends. I ask her if she can come over. She tells me that her ride is at someone else's house, but she'll have them drop her off in a little bit. A couple of hours past and she shows up. By the time, she gets over to my house a lot of the partiers have left, or they have passed out all over the house. I'm enthralled that she is there. I welcome her into the house and offer her a drink, as I am smashed from drinking all night. I take her downstairs to my room. We begin making out, and we have a special night. I've had one night with my porcelain red-haired goddess. It was the best I have ever had in my life at that time. We part ways, and I never see her again. The next day I'm back to doing drugs and alcohol.

When I met Kelly, I knew I would end up having sex with her one day. I really wanted to be her first. I wanted that because I thought of the idea of us together would be magical. And it was. I never forgot that night in my life. But I did move onto bigger and better drugs.

During this time my peers were doing Coricidin. That is an over the counter cold pill. Usually, someone would take eight or nine, and they would see things while feeling funny. One day Justin and I go to a drug store and steal many boxes of the cold pills. We grabbed as many as we could fit into out pants between the two of us. Now we were supposed to divide them up into equal shares, so we all could enjoy the trip. We pop all the little red pills out of the blister packs on to the glass stovetop of my mother's kitchen. We end up with sixty-four pills total. Ray dares me to eat all sixty-four. He was joking at the time, but when he turned away I had taken all the pills! It didn't really matter to me whether they would kill me or not. If not, I would be in for one hell of a trip! The little red pills didn't kill me, but I did have one insane trip. The next few days I was completely out of it too, but eventually, I came around. During the first following days, everything felt like I was in a room with furniture, but the background/walls were fake such as how the green screen works when the weatherman uses it during newscasts. I felt as if I was standing in an empty room with just furniture. It was all very surreal. A few months later I took another sixty-four cold pills. This time by myself hoping they would take my life from me, but my mother found me whacked out of my mind, and she took me to the hospital. I was once again admitted to the psych ward.

More time goes by and I've expanded my drug use to ecstasy, LSD, whip its (CO_2 cans), mushrooms, crack and still pot of course along with liquor and beer. My drug family now includes Lindsey, Mary, Tom, Justin, Sally, and Theodore. Mary is my on again, off again girlfriend through-out my last two years of high school. It's probably the closest thing I have had to a long-term relationship.

Lindsey was the prettier of the bunch, and she dated Tom. Mary had the bigger breasts though. Lindsey tended to flirt with me off and on, or she just tried to annoy me. We were sitting in my mother's basement/my room one day, and Lindsey kept moving my remote controls around. This was very distressing for me. I had to have my remotes parallel to each other and arranged by functionality and size. That way they could be "just right." As I was talking she would reach over and move the remote ever slow slightly. I would continue speaking while I reached down to correct the position of the remote. After this repeated several times I finally exploded, and I asked her why she had to move the remote? She replied with her long blond shoulder-length hair swinging around that she thought it was funny as she smiled that devilish smile of hers. I tell her to knock it off, but I am sure you can see some OCD traits forming in my teenage years.

I've always had a crush on Lindsay, which I felt she might have had one on me because of her constant flirting and playfulness. There were a few times we could have fooled around, but fate was not included to follow that path.

I never thought I would steal from someone to get cash for drugs or pawn something that wasn't mine. Tom and I were hanging out and it was the middle of the night. We had no more drugs or whiskey. Tom says that he knows of a lady that keeps an enormous amount of change in a gigantic jar. He claims that she leaves the window on the side of her house unlocked, and that jar is in the same room. We could go get it and cash it out at those Coin Star machines. At this time, I didn't even think this was breaking and entering, along with theft over x amount of dollars, but I thought it was normal teenage behavior. Or well normal teenage drug addict behavior. Around these same times, I was graffitiing all over St. Louis to spread my art; I never considered my art would be considered property damage as well. My graffiti name was, "Spun" as in relation to my lifestyle and how fast my world was spinning out of control. I knew it back then but I no longer cared. We go on with the heist and get the loot. Next came the cash, and it was all spent on pot and other drugs. I could escape my pain once again. I never thought it would lead to stealing a diamond from my own mother.

My father bought my mom a one-carat diamond that sat on a thin gold chain. The diamond was real because he told me that it was the only diamond he had ever purchased besides the one on my mother's ring finger. It wasn't even days later after Tom and myself spend all the loot/cash on drugs and alcohol. At the time, I had no money. I remember my father telling me about the diamond. I figured I could sell it at a pawn shop and get a big stack of cash. The pawn man tells me the diamond is real, but it is chipped. Not knowing anything about diamonds I say okay, but all I want to know is how much cash will I get. He offers seventy-five dollars. I believe retail it was a thousand. I become upset because this amount of cash is not going to get me enough drugs, but I accept without thinking about my mother, and what she would think when she discovers it missing. She never questioned me about the diamond. I've made amends to my mother about the stolen diamond, but since my family is not a family that shares heartfelt thoughts she brushes it off now 19 years later. That's one thing about my family is we Gewinner's tend to keep things in the closet. We don't air out our dirty laundry; this is how I group up in a family that is not very close.

I've blown through the cash in one day on pot, booze, and LSD. I even go onto stealing cash out of her purse, and money from the ATM machine with her Debit card. My mother would give me her card to take out twenty dollars, and bring it back to her with the receipt while leaving me with the twenty. What she didn't know was I made another withdraw for the max amount of three-hundred dollars. All this cash was used for more drugs and alcohol.

During this period of my life, my pain was unbearable against the horrid thoughts in my mind. I was in a dark place, willing to do anything to get drugs and booze to blur my vision of the life I was living. I even used crack-cocaine to numb my world.

The first time I smoked crack was on an impulse. One day I'm hanging out with Theodore, and we head to the projects where Theodore's cousins live. This area is known for where drug deals happen. Moreover, since this area is populated by black people the police pull over every white kid leaving the area and search them illegally for drugs. I've been in and out of this area so much, and I'm never caught with drugs, nor do I ever let them search me because I know my rights. The cops conclude that I have friends in this area and give up on pulling me over when I leave. I buy pot from

Theodore's cousins all the time. Moreover, I bring a lot of pot out of this area for others who can't go in there without being caught and/or arrested. One day we are standing around outside the run-down apartments, and I impulsively ask them if they got any crack on them. The cousins laugh as they think I was just joking. I'm for real, and once they realized it they quickly sold me two twenty dollars "rocks."

Theodore wonders why I'd want to start smoking crack. I respond, "Why not, what else is there to do today." I met a man in AA, and he spoke about the first time he smoked crack, but he had to stop and think about it. Did he really want to cross that line and be a crack smoker? For me, there was no line that I wouldn't cross when it came to drugs. I've even spent a whole afternoon huffing gas off a rag once. It was a substance that would alter my state of being, and I needed it altered to continue the escape of my horrid pain.

We arrive at my mother's house and start to break up the weed and crack. During this time, Sally drops by and says she is down for smoking a blunt. I negate to mention that there is crack in it. What a great person I am, huh? After we were done smoking it; I felt incredibly high, and on the same note it was like I was paralyzed as well. It eventually leaked out that Theodore and I gave Sally, who was Justin girlfriend at the time, crack. Once we were confronted about the issue and saw how everybody was extremely mad about the this, so we quickly denied it and left it at that. Our cares weren't of Sally's wellbeing, we just wanted to get high, period.

I'm out one night, as usual, chasing down booze and drugs, while getting high with my drug family. It's late into the night, and we hear the Eric aka Rico has overdosed and died at an apartment that was we used to get high at. We drive by but there are too many cops there for us to stop. While Eric was overdosing the people, there had to help him, while another group got all the drugs, plants, and other paraphernalia's out of the apartment. The cops were aware of this spot, and they even threatened them with manslaughter charges. Rico and I got high together all the time and I considered him a friend. A lot of people didn't think that he had parents, but he did. Most people thought that he was truly homeless and stayed wherever he could.

My drug family and I attended the funeral services. The services were too much for us, seeing his parents and uncles there was a shock to our system. So, we had to spend time in my car (Red Toyota) getting high ourselves smoking pot and other drugs. A lot of the girls there became livid with us doing drugs while at the funeral of someone who just overdosed. This is a sign when drugs have hold of you (me), and it becomes the only way to cope. I had problems surrounding me like tornado winds and there was no way out of the vortex.

I was unable to attend school during the second semester of my sophomore year, but I was still allowed to play hockey for the school since it was a club sport. My love of the sport began its downfall. Before I was able to show up at the rink with gusto and give it my best. Now it felt like a chore just going to practice. My hockey equipment felt as if it now weighed thousands of pounds weighing down on my shoulders. It was a true chore to play hockey on my teams at this time.

The second semester ends and for some reasons I get the same grades as I did during my first semester, but I was not present in that second semester. I spent my time getting high and causing chaos on the streets of Webster Groves. I returned for the first semester of my junior year, but I don't stick around for long, maybe one month or six weeks. I was too busy coping with my dear friend's deaths the only way I knew how, with drugs and alcohol. The second semester comes to an end.

I don't remember what I did, but around this time my mother took my cars keys away from me one night. I was pissed about this, so being the little criminal that I was I took her car keys out of her tan purse. That night I had decided I had enough and would run away. I packed my backpack with clothes and took off in her car. My goal was to drive to Arizona that night. I realized that I only had a couple grams of pot left, so I drop by Jackie's house to get some pot. I buy the pot from Jackie and decided to hang out there for a bit before I head off on my journey. Jackie was a hippie and a good friend of Katy. She was always there for me. I spent my time there smoking more pot. In addition, I had started drinking some beers too. Now I'm drunk and high, while I am about to shove off. Jackie advises me that she wished I'd stay, but it was about 2 am, and time to go. My destiny was unknown and I would make my own fate, or so I thought.

I get on the highway and then transfer onto another highway. Keep in mind at 16/17 I'm not the most highway inclined driver. Originally, I started heading off west, then north, from there I got turned around or something, and after about 30 minutes of driving I decided to get off the highway and sleep for the night, being high and drunk. I had the cruise control on, and once I got on the exit ramp I attempted to turn it off, but it would not release. Since I'm on this ramp and running out of road I figured I will just make this upcoming turn at ninety degrees while doing 60 mph. Yea, I didn't make it. The white car goes sliding across the road slamming into the median and over it. The car landed on its tires, but a cop witnessed the whole thing.

A police car comes flying up to my car lights on and sirens wailing. He flies out of his car with his gun drawn (totally unnecessary) and he began to yell at me to get out of the car. Being drunk and high at that time I couldn't figure out what had really happened. When trying to open my door the metal area of the door was bent into the front fender, thus preventing me from opening the door. Eventually, I kick the door open and get out. The jerk of a cop grabs me and throws me against my mother's car, and then proceeds to search me illegally I might add. Next, the cop takes me to the station.

While at the police station under questioning I explained what, I was doing. The cop wanted to know where I was going, and I said, "Arizona." He told me that I was in Collinsville, Illinois (heading east, not west). Arizona was west. So, he just decided to call my parents. I told the cop that my parents would beat me and such. They didn't believe me. My father had to drive my mother to the Collinsville police station. The second he walked through the door he unloaded with a verbal attack, so the cops quickly held him back. They called in a social worker to talk to me. We talked but the short of the long of it was I on the road back to Missouri with my parents. That morning I got my keys back, go figure, right? My junior year of high school is right around the corner. It's around my junior year, and I am asked what I am going to do in my life by my parents?

I'm torn at this point in my life. Everything has become so chaotic, and I'm no longer sure I want to play hockey. I tell my parents that maybe I could switch high schools and that things might be different. They agree, and my father moves into the Lindbergh school district, so I can go to school there. There is this rule that if you have played varsity for the current year and switch schools that player would have to sit out a year. I'm glad to know this because now I can focus on one team, even though my feelings towards hockey are disappearing quickly like smoke in the wind. The coach for the Lindbergh team wanted me to play for them, along with my AAA team coaches, the Hendrix brothers. This is not why I wanted to switch schools. The coaches work out a deal, so I can play my junior year if I sat out against the upcoming game against the Webster team, my old school. I'm not thrilled about this as I've already quit hockey in my mind.

While at school I meet, another kid named Chris. He has got the mad hook up for pot. I offer to sell some of this pot for Chris, and in return, I will have free pot to smoke with my profits. The selling begins and works out well. I'm smoking all day every day and drinking when I find booze. I even start ending up with some extra cash that I spend on other drugs. I started off with a quarter of a pound to sell and quickly move up to a half or pound. I'm getting mass amounts of pot to smoke too, and I'm able to keep myself stoned and drunk all day and night. Then problems start to come about.

I'm sitting around on a gloomy day (the day was a nice day out) getting high and drinking some whiskey with a few friends. It is summertime. I get a page on my purple pager reminding me that I have a summer hockey game at 4 pm. It is like 1:30 pm or something. My mother was the one who reminded me, and I tell her I don't feel like playing today. She says my father will be there, and it would be an embarrassment to him if I no-show. Not knowing yet, but I go to the last hockey game I will ever play it.

I get to the rink while I brought a few drug friends to watch me play. I put on my equipment in a very lackluster style. Thinking to myself why I am even here; it's a summer league game and the team is for shit. I take the ice to warm up skating around working the booze out of my system, while my high comes down the more I warm up. First, shift I start like always. Bam. We take the faceoff and I score a goal. As I'm skating back to center ice I decided to trip a member of the opposite team in hopes of starting a fight. No luck, but I do get a penalty. My time is over in the box, and bam I score another goal. My next shift begins, and I punch another opposing team member in the face (helmet and gloves still on). The referee gives me another penalty. When I come out of the box this time, bam I score one more goal. So as the line-mates are skating for a change I grab this guy's cage and proceed to rip it off his helmet. This player does not wish to fight. My coaches are pissed at me at this point, tell me to calm down. The last time I hit the ice I check a guy into the boards and throw a mean elbow into his face. He wants to go, so we go. In high school, hockey players aren't supposed to drop the gloves, but we do. I get five minutes for fighting, but on the way to the box I challenge the whole opposing team to a fight, and the referee throws me out of the game. My coach tells me to wait in the locker room after I am changed, but I shower and walked out of that rink with my bag on my shoulder and sticks in hand knowing that will be the last game I ever played. I had better things to do such as get drunk and stoned to numb my real pain. There was a small smile I shed as I walked out. It was like I knew, and a weight was lifted off my shoulders, like the pressure of playing hockey. Then things start to worsen then they already are in the drug game as well.

I'm home one night getting high with Alex when I get a call to sell some pot to Tom's brother. I tell him to come by, and I could sell him a couple of dimes (which is ten dollars per dime). When he gets there, he complains that the bags are too small. I say take it or leave it. He complains more and then tries to snatch the bags he was holding, which were three dimes. I grabbed him by the back of his t-shirt and yanked him back away from the door. We tussle, and a fight ensues. Tom's brother finally makes it out of the door with only one of the dimes. I basically lost ten dollars, but what I had to go through to keep twenty was a lot, and not worth it as I thought about the incident later on.

During my drug dealing times, I worked as a pizza delivery guy. One afternoon before work I take possession of three-quarters of a pound. Theodore is with me at the time. I hide the pot in my mother's house, and then take Theodore home so I can go to work. What I didn't know was that Theodore would come right back to the house and steal the massive amount of pot. I took my job as the pizza guy because at work we smoked pot all the time. I come home from work that day to find the three-quarters of a pound missing. It was stolen, and the only person who knew about it was Theodore. I know this because I got it right before work Theodore and Chris were the only ones with us. I informed Chris and he is down to find them, but that is all a false bravado. He never did anything.

That night we go out drinking to figure out what we should do about the missing pot. Instead, we all become heavily intoxicated. I pick a fight with some random kid at a party just to whip his ass. We are told that people are going to the call the cops on us, so we break out. We decided to go back to my house to drink some more. I pass out and others leave. During this same time, I was keeping some pot plants of Chris's in my basement closets. Those go missing that night too. Things are falling apart now. Chris becomes mad when we discover the pot plants missing. I guess that is what happens when you allow an addict to sell for you. He gets ripped off by his own friends, and no one wants to do anything about it. Some weeks pass by and Chris wants me to pay back the cost of the three-quarters of a pound that was given to me to sell. I'm not too keen on being a drug dealer anymore if this is all the stuff I must deal with while selling drugs to support my habit.

Weeks pass by and getting high hasn't been fun for a long time now. It felt like more of a job and recreational use. All I use it for is to numb myself from the reality that I live in. I decided once again that this world is not for me. Things had completely gotten out of control. It is a warm sunny day and I take my car, now a red Toyota and park it in my mother's garage. I close it and block the bottom of the garage with a towel. I figured the carbon monoxide will do me in. In addition, to that, I take a bottle of over the counter sleeping pills. No one was supposed to be at my mother's house that day. My pain was once again too great for me to deal with. The car is running, and I've swallowed a bottle of pills. I'm sure I will expire soon, and everything will cease for me such as my pain, sorrow, grief, sadness, frustration, disappointment, and many more feelings. I truly believe this is it for me. Only time will tell, while I wait for the carbon monoxide to take my life. For some odd reason my sister came by and she didn't even live there, but she finds my limp body in the car. She hits the grey button on the garage door opener, so fresh air can get in quickly. I am awakened by her and very frustrated as she says it's time to go back to the hospital. Again, I am admitted to the psych ward. This is something I have grown accustomed to, being admitted to the hospital, psych ward.

After I'm released from the psych ward. I tell myself that I must figure out what I'm going to do with my life. I do some hard thinking, and while I'm figuring that out I realize that I can't do it drunk. So,

I go to Alcoholics Anonymous, but that is not my first time in Alcoholics Anonymous though.

Around the time, I turned seventeen people started giving me addresses, which were to AA meetings. I had no desire to quit drinking and drugging at that time, but I thought they or something of that sorts felt I should be at these meetings.

At seventeen I'm still young and immature. These people at AA listen to me talk and tell me that it sounds like a have a problem with alcohol. I tell them I have no problem with booze, and that they are the ones with problems. I'm very hostile in these meetings towards the other AA members. Furthermore, I'm still getting drunk after the meetings, but I'm drinking by myself. Loneliness sets in as I drink away my pain.

Somehow, I get hooked up with these, "Crossroads Kids." Crossroads is a program like AA, but for people under the age of eighteen or thereabouts. They have meetings just like the AA meetings, but they are a little more open-minded about discussing my desire to quit drinking or to not quite drinking and drugging. Plus, since everybody is under eighteen I feel it is easier to share experiences and relate to them. Altogether I'm with the AA people and "Crossroads" people for a handful of weeks before I say fuck it and go back to my heavy drug and alcohol use.

Now at eighteen after my last suicide attempt with the carbon monoxide poisoning, I really should get a grip on reality. I'm no longer attending classes at school. I've secluded myself away from my friends, and I'm seeing a pretty decent psychologist on a weekly basis. Plus, she has me on one medication that I am actually taking on a regular basis, versus the cocktail of medication that I have been prescribed from previous psych ward stays. I'm back in AA again. This time I'm working a program, and I'm not hostile to the group members like before. I have a sponsor who is a pretty decent guy. Before I know it, I've made it to three months sober. I'm given my three-month coin by my sponsor. I feel that I am getting it together and things are looking up. I'm still at a loss of what to do with my life. It's like I have a grip now, but still no direction.

Since I have given up my Toyota, not driving, and I'm living at my father's house at this point in seclusion. He is the one who drives me to my weekly psych appointments. Then one day the shit hits the fan. As my father is driving me to my psychologist he suddenly blows up at me and begins yelling. I'm taken back by this. So, I respond, "How about I just join the Army?" He responds, "Are you sure?" I say, "Yea, why not." I joined the Army on a whim. I briefly discuss this with my psychologist, and she says I should take some time and review my decision. The next day I was at the recruiter's office signing papers. Yep, that is right I joined the Army on an impulse. Go big or go home, right? I never saw that psychologist again. I was off to Fort Benning Georgia for basic training within a couple of weeks of that day.

Chapter 7: The Military Years

I went to the recruiter's office to get the information I needed in order to sign up for the Army. None of the information the Army recruiter said to me really mattered; I was joining no matter what. In my mind, all I wanted to do is sign the papers and be off. I had chosen to run away from all my problems, so if that meant going to the other side of the United States, then so be it. But there were some hurdles I had to go through first.

One, I was to obtain my GED or High School Diploma. I had to take a physical exam and pass it. Lastly, I couldn't be on any medications before I joined. I didn't want to wait to finish school, because well I wasn't in school anymore for one. So, I opted to go for the GED. I found the next time a GED test would be given, and I signed up. I passed it the first time around, getting a pretty high score, I might add. I found the test unchallenging and boring. They should have given it to me just for showing up. During that same time, I took the physical and passed. Moreover, I took the ASVAP testing that would show the most likely jobs I would be suited for, combat medic was on the list of jobs for me.

I wanted the combat medic job because I figured that way I would get the medical schooling, while also getting real hands-on training with human bodies. During high school, I wanted to go to college to become a doctor or nurse, so even at a young age, I was inclined to join the medical field. If I would have slowed down a bit during my recruitment I could have found some more suitable training that would transfer into the civilian job market as the combat medic job was not much of a seller to ERs or hospitals when looking for work after I was discharged. I'll get into that later. The combat medic job is what I took.

Now I have my GED, passed the physical, and taken the ASVAP. I faced one more hurdle to leap over. The Army has a rule that no one can join the military while on any medication. A person could go off the medication and join in six months. Then after basic training and AIT, one could go back on any medications they were on before. I didn't want to wait the six months, so the recruiter having no medical knowledge tells me to list medications as none. Keep in mind the medication that I am on now is a psychiatric medication, and this recruiter guy just tells me to stop it without checking with my psychologist or doctor. They'd do anything to get someone to sign up. It was all a matters of numbers. It didn't really matter to me, because I went on and off medications all the time in the past two years without consulting anybody, except myself. Everything is all wrapped up and basic training here I come.

My basic training was at Fort Benning, Georgia (home of the infantry).

This basic training wasn't co-ed like some basic training are across the U.S. When I joined the Army they had a motto of the "Nicer, Kinder, Army," but for the drill sergeants at Benning, it was still the type of training that the men got in the early nineties. That meant they worked the crap out of us, we went through the old school training. No mercy.

When I started basically I had three months sober and by the time I finished, I had around six months sober. While being three months sober at the start of basic I didn't have to deal with any withdraw symptoms, nor did I not suffer from my usual insomnia. Insomnia plagued me since I was a little kid. Mainly my insomnia started after I'd watched Nightmare on Elm Street, with Freddy Krueger and all, but long after Freddy was gone from my nightmares I was still plagued like the impoverished and poor in Somalia.

I was too busy to think about drinking during basic, but when our days were long and nights short there is not much time to think about drinking or anything for that matter, but being three months sober helped me greatly. My insomnia was cured, because when we were putting in sixteen-hour days, and doing hard labor and exercise, plus schooling. I was so worn out that when I hit my rack (bunk) I passed out immediately knowing I would be up in just hours if they didn't decide to wake us up earlier. I believe my mental health was non-existent during this period.

At the start of basic training in my teens; I was self-medicating with booze and drugs during that time. I feel all the hard work with training and all, it exhausted me from having any symptoms if I did have any they were masked by the high levels of testosterone that would go along with a group of men in basic training.

Personally, I thought basic training was a breeze if you picked up on what was taught very fast and had the capacity to push yourself beyond your normal limits. I did fine when pushing myself due to my hockey regimen of training that I did on my own with the goal to be the very best while attempting to reach the NHL level. Then they gave us weapons too.

Being handed an M-16 and only given a brief instruction on how to use it is a powerful thing because we were firing real bullets, and anything could have happened. I qualified on the M-16 my first time around. That is done by hitting X number of targets out of Y number of targets with only Z number of bullets. Next, we handled live grenades. On the grenade range, it was very surreal, because we had on flak jackets, and once that pin was pulled if it slipped out of my hand on the inside of the solid brick wall it would be the end of me. Having attempted suicide before it never crossed my mind to take myself out during basic training. I threw both of my grenades and qualified expert with them. Most of us did though. Basic training came and went very fast.

I learned quite a few things during my training at Fort Benning. Besides learning how to push myself and continue forward I learned how to develop trust amongst others who I barely knew. That is something that I lost quickly after leaving the Army. I learned how to be comfortable in uncomfortable situations, such as when I had sand down my pants or up my back from low crawling and such. Meaning that during combat I wouldn't be able to stand up and dust myself off or laying in a position unable to move for hours upon hours. I just had to deal with the discomfort. I had formed tight bonds with other members of my platoon, some who I am still in contact with to this very day. Some of the others had been murdered and committed suicide.

We were days away from graduation, and it felt like we had just started. Due to the excessive heat in Georgia, we were allowed to wear our class B's. That uniform is the dark green dress pants and short-sleeve light green dress shirt. The class A uniform would be the dress pants and dark green suit type of jacket. You might have seen this uniform in some movies involving the Army where the Generals and Majors are wearing what is a dark green suit. In addition, to all their ribbons and achievements on the breast area of their uniform.

Graduation day is here and my mother and father along with my niece (she was about 3 or 4 years old) came down to Georgia to see me graduate. We marched out on the parade area, while our parents and family sat on elevated bleachers. We stopped in formation. There I was standing at parade rest wearing my uniform, and on my breast area, I wore the ribbon for completing basic training and below that, I had my M-16 and Grenade medals showing I had qualified with both of those weapons. During the graduation ceremonies, there were some speeches made about various things about being in the Army and such. In the end, our parents could come down and greet us, while after that we could spend the day with them.

My parents approached me, and I hugged my mom and niece. When I went to greet my father, he was able to get the words out that he was proud of me. He also began to tear up, which is something I have never seen this man do before. His regular persona would be that of a hardened man with no emotions. It was a surreal experience to see my father cry tears of joy. Basic training is officially over.

The next day we are sent off to the airport to report to our AIT assignments, which I believe stood for Advanced Individual Training. Mine would be at Fort Sam Houston, Texas. That was where my medical training would begin. We did have one hell of a time getting to Fort Sam Houston though.

It is me and a handful of other soldiers that left my basic training and we're going to Texas for medical school. Our flight was delayed due to bad weather. Some of the guys tried and use their military Ids to buy beers at the bar in the airport. It worked, and the bartender sold to them. Hours have passed many of the men are now drunk. I was able to keep my sobriety during this airport experience. Eventually, our plane arrives, and the sober men are carrying the drunk ones on board to sleep it off during the flight. They carried them in the firemen carry. We make it to Texas and disembark the plane.

At the airport, we retrieve our luggage, and since we missed the van that was supposed to pick us up; we had to call the main desk at Fort Sam Houston to ask for a ride. They tell us to get a cab. We finally arrive at the base and are directed to sleep in empty barracks. We are told that we will be directed in the morning where to report for AIT.

I'm in Echo company for my medical schooling, which means that everybody in that company would be there for the same reasons, medical school. AIT is a lot different from basic training, here the drill instructors treat you like human beings! The handful of men and myself that came from Benning (home of the infantry) were used to being dropped; that means when we were dropped one would have to get down and do anywhere from twenty-five to one hundred push-ups. Like I said AIT was different. First, we were now with female soldiers so being around all men for a few months the females defiantly caught our attention. When it came to push-ups the Benning boys were not team players.

The drill instructors here would drop soldiers for like ten or fifteen push-ups. The Benning boys thought this was a joke. Furthermore, in basic when one soldier was dropped we all got down in support. When being dropped in a group that group of soldiers count off in a cadence, but during our basic we learned to never go above zero, showing we can take whatever is put out, no matter what or for how long; hints staying at zero. After a while these easier drill instructors keep the count going and said we would not be done until the group hit ten. Again, the Benning boys refused to go up in the count. Our voices overpowered the others so we were heard, and not the rest of the group. The women would constantly yell out for us, "To be a team player", but we would not give out showing we could take any grueling punishment that would be given out. Eventually, the drill instructors separated the rest of the company from the Benning boys, and we formed our own platoon, ready to take on anything. We were constantly in the front leaning rest (push-up) position all the time. The women were very happy to see this happen. Afterward, none of the women were willing to go on dates with us though. Go figure, right?

In basic training, we did not have access to our civilian clothes. In AIT we did, and our days ended at 5 pm. That meant we could go off the post and into town to do whatever we please, hints the women not willing to spend their free time with the over pumped testosterone filled Benning boys.

Given that we spent most of our time in classrooms learning at an accelerated pace. Many people had to spend their free time studying as we could go through two to three textbook chapters in one day and be tested on them the next. The Combat Medic course was listed as the 91-Bravo, which later changed to 91-Whiskey. This schooling had a high dropout and failure rate, due to its accelerated pace. One would either learn it or not. The material for some reason was easy for me to grasp, and I passed my exams with flying colors. During my free time, my sobriety is shaken.

My friends (the Benning boys) and I usually just ran around post after 5 pm trying to pick up on women or convince the ones I were in class with to sleep with us on the weekend. Since during basic, we were cuddled up with each other (men) in the freezing cold nights in Georgia. It was the weekends that people in Echo company stayed in hotel rooms drinking and fucking. It is Friday after 5 pm, and I choose to hang out with some buddies running around San Antonio, with the mindset of staying at one of the hotel rooms that are booked for the weekend, in hopes of getting laid. Besides hooking up with the females at the hotel parties people just drank, and that made hooking up much easier. I'm six months sober maybe seven by now, but I'm not working a program, nor am I speaking to my sponsor from back home.

I arrive at one of the hotel rooms a little after 8 pm, and the party is in full swing. I figured I could just decline any alcohol offered to me, which I did the first two or three times, but on the fourth time I said, "Fuck it, why not?" Go big or go home, right? Relapse happens when a person is not doing two things in his sobriety. One, working some sort of program, and two, talking with his sponsor on an almost daily basis, even if it is just to check in. I was doing neither, and I relapsed that quickly. It would be another twelve years before I got sober again. I got smashed and laid that night, but I don't remember much. Before I knew it, I was dying for the weekend to come so I could drink freely.

After my initial drinking episode, all I could think about is getting my next beer or whiskey. The next weekend came, and I went out with my friend Elliot. We ran around town and ate at Hooters. Obviously hitting on the gorgeous waitresses while we had some beers and ate our food. Since we couldn't find anything to really do in the middle of the day, we went to a strip club.

The club was empty except one other guy or so was in the club. There were about four or five strippers working during the daytime shift. We got plenty of attention from the strippers, and one said she was about to get off soon. Then she asked us if we wanted to hang out at her place. We agree and follow her home, but not without picking up some Bud Light and Jim Beam. It was everything a guy could ask for hanging out at a stripper's place. When we arrived, she changed into lingerie; it was black and lacey while being see-through as well. We couldn't believe our eyes, but we were very okay with it considering she was a twelve out of ten on the gorgeous scale. We begin drinking, and she wants to know if it would be cool if she invited some friends over? They were female, and of the same free-spirited in keeping clothes on. It was like being in the Playboy mansion minus Hugh Hefner and the mansion. These women had no problem hanging out in their bras and panties while we all drank and chit-chatted the day away. It was heaven! When nightfall hits they all want to go to a club.

All of us take a couple of cars and head out to the club. The women are dressed up and all looked gorgeous. At the current time, I've consumed quite the amount of beer and a decent amount of whiskey, but that doesn't stop me from drinking at the club. By the end of the night, I am pretty smashed because I can only remember bits and pieces of the evening. I don't remember why but Elliot and I had to be back at the barracks that night, so the girls drop us off on post.

I'm helped to my bunk by Elliot, and I pass out. I defiantly would have failed a sobriety test at this point like ten times over. Elliot being a nice guy and all decides to keep watch over me. I'm passed out on my back at this point. Sometime in the middle of the night, I had thrown up, but since I am on my back I keep it in my mouth and gurgle the vomit as it has no place to go. During our medical classes, we learn that this does obstruct one's airway. Elliot hears the gurgling and checks on me. I'm lucky enough Elliot paid attention in class, and he turns me onto my side so the vomit can drain out of my mouth. If he wasn't there at that point I would have died by affixation of my own vomit. Someway to go out, huh? It was just another time I cheated death like all my other suicide attempts, but I wasn't in a suicidal mindset when I was drinking that night, it was the alcoholic in me that needed to consume that much booze that night, plus some. Or any night for that matter too little is not enough and too much is still not enough either. Most would think this event would be enough to scare them to slow down. For me, no not one bit, I moved forward without a hesitant step.

By the end of AIT, we had to pass and be certified in CPR, have our EMT license, and be IV certified. In addition, the very last part was a two-week field exercise where our new-found skills were to be put to the test. If we passed then only we would be graduating. There were a handful of people that made it to the field exercise but couldn't perform the necessary medical tasks on live people. They would be "recycled", which meant they would have to wait for the next class to start, but they would be starting from the beginning. So just book smarts didn't guarantee that you would graduate. I pass everything with minimal effort while spending my off time drinking away my occult pain.

Graduation came and went. My parents didn't come to this one as they had the thought of we just took a trip to Georgia to see you graduate from basic training a few months ago. During the course of AIT, we learned much medical information and were able to put it into practice. Some of the things we learned were: basic first aid, advanced first aid, trauma and emergency treatment, pre-hospital life support (advanced), along with how to treat the injured during a chemical attack, CPR, IV sticks, blood draws, and much more all in the course of three months or under. I'm not kidding when I say it was an accelerated medical course. The official title was Medical Specialist Course. Once AIT was finished I went back to St. Louis for a few weeks for leave (vacation) before I headed to my assignment posting at Fort Lewis, Washington.

When I arrived in Washington and reported for duty I was sent to the reception area before being assigned a unit. I stayed there for about a week. Then I was assigned to the 1st of the 5th Infantry Battalion. My buddy from basic and AIT Andrew and I were sent to the same unit. So, I had a friend. We hauled our gear over to our new unit. At that time, our unit was on a field exercise, and they wouldn't be back for a few days. We get assigned temporary rooms and are told that we will be moved in with the other medics once the unit gets back.

After a handful of days or so our unit returns from the field. We meet the other medics and get situated in the platoon. The guys grill us with medical questions to see if we know our shit or not, but both Andrew and I impress them greatly. I'm told within a week or so that I will be a line medic. What that means is me the medic will be attached to one infantry platoon (about 25-30 men), and it will be my job to take care of those men in combat, field exercises, on ranges (rifle, pistol, etc.), and so forth. Not many medics make it on the line. One would have to really know their stuff to stay with an infantry platoon. A lot of medics get sent back before the end of their first field exercise. I was attached to Bravo company 2nd platoon, and I stayed with them my whole time I was in service. Hints I knew my shit and knew it well. What makes a good line doc is they must be able to do everything the infantrymen do, plus their own job. Some medics try to get by doing only their jobs, but as I loved to do the things my infantry guys did, such as ropes course, firing ranges, clearing rooms, and more, plus my job as well; they respected me more than the medic just trying to get by. When you have your infantry men's respect they will go above and beyond for you, no matter what. Even if they have to take a bullet for you because they will count on you saving their own life with the bullet in them and not you. The key is trust in this type of situation. My infantry men trusted me to keep them alive if they were ever shot, injured, and hurt. I had their respect and they had my trust to keep me from sustaining injury.

 Living in this high testosterone environment, when the common thing is to drink and smoke it doesn't matter if you are not twenty-one yet. Most of the older soldiers see it as if your old enough to die for this country than your old enough to drink a beer. Drinking was encouraged in our unit. When soldiers are drunk, fights will ensue.

I had given up on my sobriety and was drinking around the clock, except during training. The other men were doing that as well. My alcoholism was easily hidden in this environment since drinking was the norm around the barracks. One night my roommate, Brandon and I along with some others are drinking some Coronas in our room.

We had been drinking for some time now, and the trash can was filled up with clear empty bottles. Then we started putting the empties on the window sill. Brandon gets the bright idea to start pissing in the empty bottle on the window sill, but we complain that they will start to smell. He then proceeds to put the piss filled bottles back into our mini-fridge where the fresh Coronas are. This irritates me greatly. We argue back and forth. Eventually, a fight pursued between Brandon and me, but even though we were beating the crap out of one

another it was a fight that more or less
would be a disagreement between brothers.
That was what we were brothers in arms.
The fisticuffs ended in mutual agreement,
and the next morning we go out to breakfast
at Denny's as friends with no bad blood
between us. That's just how things were
done in our unit. The following Monday
didn't fly so well with our platoon sergeant.

That Monday information our
platoon sergeant cruised by us and stopped.
As he stood there looking at Brandon and I
and us standing there looking right back at
him with each of us sporting a black eye.
He says what happened to you two. We
quickly explained we got into a bar fight,
and that he should see the other guys. He
buys that, and responds as did they know we
were Army or did they know our names, and
were the cops called? We answer no to all
the questions. The higher ups didn't really
care about us young men getting into bar
fights as long as we couldn't be made.

By the end of the day, our platoon
sergeant finds out what really happened as
men in the Army are worse than a lady's

sewing circle. Our platoon Sargent doesn't condone this type of behavior, and our punishment is that he ties us together with three feet of 550 cord (rope). Since there was no bad blood between Brandon and I we ended up having fun being tied together. We would close-line people walking in-between us and what not. So, it is not even the middle of the next day before our platoon sergeant gives in and unties us. Then there were the bar fights when all the guys fought on the same side.

I went out to the bar to do some drinking and bonding with my infantry platoon, about ten of the guys were there that night. We all headed out to a local bar in town. There were drinking and dancing. I had quite a few drinks already before we left for the bar, but in the military, most of us drank in excess, so a few of the other guys had some drinks beforehand too. Hints we were already drunk before we walked into the bar. That is one thing men in the military (me included) could do, hold our booze. We were trained professionals when it came to drinking.

We arrive at the bar, and as we walk in all of us are looking around to see where the hot girls were at. If they had boyfriends with them it didn't matter. After doing a quick scan of the place we headed up to the bar to get some drinks. I ordered a beer and a shot to start. As the guys and I get liquored up I feel the urge to dance. I get on the dance floor and begin to dance; I'm drunk so I could care less how foolish I look.

My first dance was with two girls that were dancing together, and it was quite fun. One was a blond and the other a brunette. Both had long flowing hair and was of the slim body type with medium size breasts. It was the best sandwich I could have ever been in, with two hot chicks bumping and grinding against me for the better part of ten minutes. I had a few more dance partners, but sooner than later I hit up the bar for some more drinks. As I waited for my drinks I begin chatting up some girl who was waiting for her drinks. She said she had a boyfriend, but I told her that didn't matter. The other guys had scattered across the bar all in search of some tail. Then this chick's boyfriend walks up and becomes all defensive and such. I tell him he should relax, because if he has a faithful girlfriend than there is nothing to worry about. Then I laughed ever so slightly. My thoughts were this guy has no clue of the back up I brought to the bar with me, being my infantrymen.

To all men out there if your girlfriend is willing to talk with another man at a place where you and he are spending time together she one, wants to see you get into a fight, and two, to see if you will win, and three, to see if you trust her enough to enjoy the company of a potential friend. Most women just want to see how you will react. Back to the bar story.

I grow bored and annoyed with this boyfriend and his male masochist. I asked the girl to hit the dance floor with me. She gladly accepts my offer, and we push past the boyfriend. The girl and I take our drinks to the dance floor. We are dancing for a few minutes or so.

Remember when I told you how if you're a good doc the infantry guys will do anything for you and protect you no matter what, and I was a great doc to my guys. The girl and I are dancing, and the boyfriend decides to get all alpha male on me, which is a bad idea when that guy (me) has ten of his infantrymen with him, and those guys are trained killers (alpha male times 100) who trust their doc completely in keeping them alive if they are injured. So, nothing can or will happen to their doc. That is just their mindset when it comes to the doc, not to mention they do enjoy fighting too.

The boyfriend moves across the dance floor undetected by me, but not by my men. By the time the guy gets about three feet from me, and a few of my guys noticed. These are also my buddies who had to witness my earlier interaction with the boyfriend. This guy can't even raise his fist back to cheap-shot me from behind before about three of my guys pull him back and jump on him. My other guys noticed this and jump in as they begin to stomp him. I spin around to see what's going on, and I noticed it is that guy again; getting his ass whipped. I look back at the girl and laugh, she just smiles back. After about a minute or two some of my guys hear that they are calling the cops. One guy tells me this, and I tap my men and say it's time to go and go now! I turn back to the girl and say it was nice to meet you and to call me, even though she doesn't have my number; I smile at her with a smug look on my face. We all quickly gather and break out like a ghost vanishing in a darkened hallway. The boyfriend has no clue what hit him. That was his mistake.

Afterward, my guys are all key up after beating the boyfriend down. Remember our higher-ups don't care about the bar fights if we leave before the cops show up, and no one knows our names. This was a successful exit strategy from the bar, and not one of us has a mark to prove we were in that fight. I remember watching the boyfriend getting stomped, and all I could think was what an unfortunate bastard to get his ass kicked so bad, especially in front of his own girlfriend. For one, he knew I was military and any guy in the military knows a thing or two about hurting another human, even if we slept through the classes on hand to hand combat; it is drilled into us on a daily to weekly bases. You will learn something eventually.

When you live on a military post, and the town that is right outside of the post; that is a military town. To the civilians of that town, all of us stick out like a sore thumb. It's mainly our haircuts, but not many are willing to mess with us or attempt to start trouble. I would think after the fact that guy was not surprised to get his ass whipped, but there are always the guys who think they are tough enough to take on the proud.

There is a saying in the Army that we work hard and play even harder. What that means is we spend everyday training in some form or the other, plus we are constantly going on field exercises. Field exercises are when we spend two to three weeks in the field rarely getting any sleep, and no showers. There are a few guys who are injured and cannot attend these field exercises. Those guys jobs are to have coolers full or beer and liquor bottles ready for us when we come back. We always walk out to the exercise point and walk back too. So, it could be a Thursday and we just walked twenty miles into our barracks, and there would be booze waiting for us. Generally, we drank while we cleaned our weapons until they were good enough to be turned into the armory. Then we would stow our gear, and be ready to hit the bars in a few hours. Work hard, play harder. Drinking was what was expected out of us when we came out of a field exercise. It was just a way of life, but for me, it hid my true alcoholism, and the pain I was suffering inside. I never shared my true thoughts with any of my Army buddies. I kept them buried inside me as a coffin gets put into the ground, never to be exposed. The more I drank the deeper I could push my pain into the dark side of the abyss in my life.

After a couple of years at my station, I met my soon to be my wife, but that was just a drug and alcohol-fueled marriage. The guys and I one night are out drinking at a club on the post and I meet this one lady named Maggie. We sleep together on the first night and then begin to date. After a few weeks, she had a party at her place, and her friend comes over. This lady is so hot and gorgeous, her name is Crystal. She has my attention right away. As the night proceeds forward I constantly pull her away from the party, so we could be alone. I tell her that I'd rather be with her then with her friend (my current girlfriend). Eventually, I get her to start making out with me, and before I know it my current girlfriend comes in search of me, what a pest. She catches us; then I have to go talk with her about my actions, and when she becomes upset I use that as a reason to break up. After that, I run back to Crystal and presumed my desire to be with her. On that same night we sleep together, and the jerk that I am we use my most recent girlfriend's bed, go figure. I didn't even think about how this would affect my ex-girlfriend all I cared was that I was getting laid by Crystal.

Now I am dating Crystal and a few weeks go by. I get the bright idea to get married because when a soldier is married he gets extra money to cover housing costs and living expenses. Up next is the proposal. I call Crystal and invite her to the barracks because I want to ask her something important. She says that she will be on her way. I realize that I couldn't propose marriage sober, so I head to the gas station on post and buy three to four 40 ounce bottles of beer (yes, they still sold those back then). I make it back to the barracks and begin drinking my first one. This is probably a sign that this marriage won't go over well if I must get drunk before I propose. I get about two-thirds through the second one and Crystal arrives at the barracks. She comes up to my room, and we make out a bit. She wants to know what I wanted to ask her? I tell her that I have to get through this second bottle and start the next one first. "Flashing warning sign; this is a bad idea."

As that happens I start explaining in a rapid fashion (as I was probably manic at this point) that the Army will pay me more money if I was married and such. After going in rapid circles for about ten minutes or so I finally ask if she will marry me?

After a slight pause, she says, "Yes." Woo Hoo extra money here I come is my only thought. Another bad sign.

We have sex on my bed for an hour or two. Then we decide to leave the barracks and go back to her place to have more sex and celebrate our engagement, but not without more liquor though. We take separate cars so I can drive back on post in the morning for work. We never make it off post though. I get pulled over for swerving by an MP (military police) and receive a DUI. Not the best start to getting engaged. Also, not my last DUI either. My now fiancé heads home, and I spend the rest of that night sitting in a military police station waiting for my first sergeant to pick me up in the morning. All I can think while waiting is so much for more sex huh. I even blame my fiancé for my DUI since it was her idea to leave and go to her place. I regret ever getting in my car that night.

The next morning comes and goes along with the next day. I figured it would be a couple of months before we actually tied the knot, but before the weekends she calls me and says to bring a friend to be a witness for our wedding, and to be there at 6:30 pm. She gives me the address of a minister that can perform the wedding ceremony, and do the wedding certificate. Of course, I grab my buddy Andrew and a bottle of whiskey too. Another sign the wedding is off to a great start. Really, I just should be drunk about 16 hours out of the day to function. I lived my life in an alcoholic fog during this time in my life.

I met her at the guy's address, and it is a hippy looking dude who is one of those guys who became ordained online. He also performs the ceremony in his mom's back room, who he still lives with. Luckily, I have a few shots of whiskey in me, and I'm not becoming weirded out by all this. He performs the ceremony without a hitch, and we say our, "I do's", even though we don't have rings yet. Me and my now wife fuck later on that evening, which is the foundation of our marriage. Fucking and then eventually the fighting came about.

The wedding certificate gets turned into the Army so I can be paid more cash and what not. My now wife jumps on the ball and finds us a nice apartment not too far from post. Next, we go ring shopping. Keep in mind that I am drunk for most of this, still thinking I would live in the barracks for a few more months. We pick out her and my ring, but her credit is for shit and mine is great. I buy both of our wedding rings. We move into our apartment and make it our own. Things went well at first, but that didn't last for long.

As I mentioned before this marriage was a drug and alcohol-fueled marriage. My wife and I did a lot of drinking during the nights as we set up our apartment and shopped for furnishings for our place. We played nice at first; it was all fun and fucking. My wife on evenings even tried to be the good wife with offering to cook me dinner and what not. I didn't get it when she would ask me what I wanted for dinner, and I'd replied, "Oh, I'll have just a few beers." Until she had to spell it out for me as, "I will cook whatever you desire to eat if you tell me what you want." The weekends are where we would do our serious partying.

Crystal had a friend who was gay and worked at a party supply store. He was also into the rave scene, and he sold ecstasy in his spare time. It wasn't long before my wife and I were doing ecstasy on the weekends and hitting raves. The "E" fueled our sex life even more. Plus, the partying kept increasing, we drank, did "E", and I started smoking pot. My fellow soldiers were doing drugs with me. Yes, this happens in the military, unfortunately. There are two things I learned when you run away from your problems and go all the way across the United States. One is your problems with eventually show up at your new location sooner than later. Two was that I was not the only guy to think of joining the Army to run away from their problems. Some of them had drug and alcohol problems like me. When you put a bunch of dry drug and alcohol addicts together it won't be long before they start seeking out drugs together. You may be thinking guys in the military are on drugs? Well not all of them, but the ones who joined for reasons like me could. Addiction, it is cunning, baffling, and powerful. One would be surprised what an addict will do to obtain their drug of choice.

My wife and I are on drugs and booze. We are constantly fucking and fighting. Fighting and fucking. Then about two months into the marriage, she cheated on me. Crystal slept with one of my military buddies while we were partying one night, and I was asleep (well passed out) in our bedroom. I was pissed about this, but then again, the drugs and alcohol clouded and numbed me from going into a rage. That rage was just being bottled up and shoved down deep inside me. Christmas was right around the corner.

I decided to fly home for Christmas that year and spend some time with my family. When I arrived home my family was shocked to find out I had gotten married. They noticed the ring on my finger. A lot of them were wondering why they weren't invited to the wedding, but I explained to them that it was a quick and cheap wedding. They followed up with is she pregnant, and I said, "No." Christmas was coming to an end.

I flew home and it wasn't a week or so before the incident happened. We were out partying at a friend's house that night; drinking and doing drugs obviously. As the party progressed I couldn't find her. After looking around the house for a while I decided to go outside, and I found her coming out of the house from across the street. Her clothes were disheveled and hair all messy. She had slept with a guy at the party who lived across the street. I was livid. I then began to yell and scream at her. After I was done yelling I took off and went back to our apartment leaving her there stranded.

At home, I was drunk and high with a spinning mind. What proceeds next was a slew of phone calls back and forth. The calls contained vague threats, but it was the only way I knew at that time on how to express my feelings and betrayal. She pleaded with me and such saying it wasn't how it looked, and that I was over-reacting. I was still enraged, and I hung up the phone for that last time. Next, I turned it off, so I would not take any more calls from my wife. Given the fact, I was still very smashed, but due to my rage, I decided to grab a beer out of the fridge to calm down. I drank my beer and hit the sack. The cats were alive and well when I passed out. My wife must have gotten a ride home later.

I wake up some hours later to my wife screaming saying that cats were dead. In a state of confusion, I could barely understand her, comprehend what was going on. If you have ever been so drunk that you pass out and are woken up just hours later it is hard to even know where you are at, or what's going on. I know that is how it usually is for me. As I partly come to grips with where I'm at I become enraged once again because I told her not to come home as she was not welcome here anymore. Push came to shove and I briefly choked my wife. The cops showed up, and I was arrested while being taking off to jail. My thoughts at this time were I messed up big and how can I get out of this. What would happen in jail?

The jail was a joke or at least county jail was. By that I mean these harden supposedly criminals were just regular guys who had made a mistake at that time in their life. I hired a lawyer to make all the charges go away, but all he did do was rip me off for ten thousand dollars. The official charge that I pled to was assault three, and I did sixty-three days out of ninety days in jail. I turned twenty-one in jail but was released shortly after my twenty-first birthday.

I'm living back in the barracks. Due to the felony, I had the option of leaving the Army early, which I took. I figured it would be no point in me staying in the same state as my soon to be ex-wife. Mentally I had a lot on my mind such as trying to figure out what I want to do in life.

What better thing to do than drink away my problems. That is exactly what I did. While waiting for my discharge paperwork to come through I drank, mainly alone in my room. I was twenty-one so I could buy my own alcohol without any issues. It didn't really matter if I showed up for formation in the morning, so I spent my evenings drinking to excess. I tried to deep-six my pain with alcohol as a coping mechanism. This only pushed my problems down more and more. Eventually, they would fight their way back up and reck more havoc then I would have if I dealt with them then.

On the weekend, my Army buddies drank with me. Remember when I said that a lot of guys joined the military with drug and alcohol problems. It didn't take much drinking before we needed something else. So, I got some pot and following that was coke and shrooms. Despite trying to drink away my problems whenever I sobered up they were still there, thus causing myself to pick up another bottle of beer.

I spent the last few months of my military career in a drunken haze. The only positive thing I did was take a class on how to write the perfect resume and how to act during a job interview. A discharge date comes about, and I am given a one-way bus ticket back to the dreaded town of St. Louis. I could have driven, but I had totaled my decked-out Honda Civic in the last month I was in Washington. I drove it into a lake, and I was drunk at the time, go figure, right? That car was my baby though, and I was deeply saddened to have lost her. The day comes, and I am on the bus all the way across the country once again running from my life's problems in hopes that they do not follow. They follow through.

Chapter 8: The Return to St. Louis and My 20's in Years

I arrive late one night in St. Louis on my cross-country bus, the night is dark as my future would turn out to be. It was like a flashing warning sign before a cliff. My father picks me up in his black Ford SUV. I think it was an explorer. I was dropped off in the city of St. Louis. When my father picked me up, and we headed back to his apartment since it was late, around midnight, and my reunion with my family would be held the next day.

The reunion started around noon, and we had a barbecue. Everything seemed fine and okay, but I didn't feel right being there. I was uncomfortable in my own skin. On a positive side, there were no family fights, which is great, because normally they were started by me, and then I would take off, refusing to come back. A couple of weeks go by, and I'm living off the money that I had in the bank before I left the Army. In addition, to the check, the insurance company had given me when I wrecked my Honda Civic before I left for St. Louis.

My stuff that was shipped home from the military arrived in those couple of weeks. I get settled in; now I'm living in my mother's basement. It's time to find a job and secure a car to get myself to and from work. Since I had no incoming money I decided to buy my sister's 93 Accord for one thousand dollars, since she was in the market for a new car, and she could sell me hers outright. That way I wouldn't have a car payment to cover each month.

The car was a black four-door 93 Honda Accord. I wanted to trick it out, but I didn't have the cash to do it fully like my Civic was, but I did put a CD player in the car along with three twelve inch JL Audio subwoofers and a Soundstream amplifier. The car and system got me along just fine, and everybody could hear me coming from afar. I did love my Honda Civic though and longed for another car just like it; all decked out and what not.

My Honda Civic was originally white. It was a four-door sedan, and a five-speed transmission, stick. I bought the car while I was in St. Louis on vacation, and drove it up to Washington state with the help of my father; it was a father/son type of trip, and things didn't go bad either. Really, I just needed him to help drive the distance, because back then I fell asleep in the car a lot on long distance trips. We arrived at Fort Lewis without a hitch. We stopped in Glacier National Park and Mount Rushmore to do some sightseeing on our cross-country trip. That way the trip would be worth it and my father could do some of the driving. I did enjoy being able to experience those two parks during my lifetime because during my career of drinking I missed out on a lot of trips I could have taken due to the monster of a grip alcohol had on me. The time in the car was nice though.

I've always been a car person with having stereo systems in every car I've had since Jeremy's dad gave me Jeremy's old system from the car he died in. That act meant a lot to me, especially because it was Jeremy's and the first system I ever had.

I believe the first subs I had in my Civic where two twelve-inch subwoofers (Rockford Fosgate) and the same brand of amp. Once in Washington, I added an eight-ball gear shifter, and a blue neon lighting hook up; this was before they had come out with LED lighting. My desire to change the look of my car came after watching the first Fast and the Furious movie. After seeing that movie, I swapped out the front and back bumpers and changed the side skirts as well with a kit, including the front and back bumpers. Lastly, I switch the front fenders with ones that had three slots in them, even with the engine compartment. Then I had the car painted midnight blue. I found some white tail lights that would go great with the midnight blue paint job, so I swapped them out as well. I put a cold air intake on the engine, so I could have a little more horsepower. Lastly, I swapped out my exhaust with a chrome one which had a bigger pipe. In total and in under one year I spend around three thousand dollars into improving my car. I even took apart the dash and hand painted it a blue and white color scheme, along with painting the inside of my headlights white. My original system was not the only system I kept in my car. I believe it went through three different sets of amps and subs. It was my baby, and I ended up totaling it out before I could take it back to St. Louis. I was drinking at the time I wrecked my car.

I did show my car off on the waterfront in Seattle. Me and another army buddy of mine were both into cars. He drove a two-door baby blue Honda Civic as he had his all decked out as well. We would constantly race each other up and down the highway and around town with our cars. It was a cool thing to have a hot car because that meant it got the girls attention too. I felt so cool for once and felt I belong in the car scene.

I'm back in St. Louis done with my time in the military driving an old 93 Honda Accord. At least I have a system in it though. Next, I must find a job as I'm running out of money that I saved to live off before I found a job. I did spend a lot of that cash on beer and booze while awaiting my discharge date thought. I'd often miss formations in the morning due to hangovers and over drinking the night before. Usually, those were times when I was drinking alone too. This is something the constantly reoccurs throughout my life. Loneliness, pain, sadness, and melancholy. I was surrounded in turmoil like a twister holding me in the vortex.

I'm settled in and on the job hunt. I go on several interviews, but I'm told my military qualifications don't mean squat without having a nursing degree or even an MD. This is very discouraging for me to hear. Here I am having done many procedures and medical treatments in the field, which means in the dirt while keeping my patients' infection free. Not to mention I worked mainly in the dark with little to no light, and I'm being told that I need to obtain a piece of paper to get a job in an ER or get a nursing degree. My melancholy begins to set in at this time, as alcohol forms it's grips on me. My whole point of joining the Army was to get the classroom schooling along with real live hands-on training, and now I can't use those skills in the job market. I was very frustrated. At the time, I'm drinking around two to four twenty-four ounce cans of beer a night, and maybe a little more on the weekends.

Frustrated with the outlook of my job search I decided that maybe I will just go back to school and get a nursing degree. I made an appointment with a college consular to discuss how I could pre-sue my nursing degree and having my military schooling transferred into college credits. That way I would not have to take classes over again that I've already passed with flying colors. The consular then told me that none of my military schoolings would transfer except maybe a gym credit from the time I spend in basic training. This is just unfathomable, and all I can do is wait for a breaking point in the conversation to say okay and leave while telling her I would be in touch. My drinking increases more after this episode. As my depression builds and the outlook seemed bleak it is only feasible to increase my drinking. Alcohol finally makes its full solid grip on me by this point. I didn't mind, because I needed something to dull my pain and reality that surrounded me and my life, but I wasn't fully aware of alcohols grip on me just yet.

During this time, I try to reach out to a few high school buddies, but I'm unsuccessful, and they don't return my calls. I'm now left alone with my beer and discouraging job search. Right, when I was just out of money I get a job offer to work in a family practice office, and I take it with gusto. I'm paid ten dollars an hour, which I didn't really care about the amount I was paid; I just wanted a job. I thought things were going well during my first three months, but when I was at my new job for about three weeks I get another job offer from a previous interview. I decline it since I had just started at this new job, but later on, down the line, I regretted it greatly. It turns out the first job only kept people that didn't want the benefits, health and dental. If you did want them, they canned you after three months when the probationary period was over, which they did to me and many others as well. It's back to the job search.

I was not having any luck getting interviews for medical offices, and I needed to have some money coming in, so I took a job at a Shell gas station working the register and what not. During this time, I had gotten into doing sleight of hand magic, so while things were slow at the register I would practice my card tricks, and whatnot on customers and other employees. It was a lot of fun. As I had some money coming in from my job at Shell I wasn't hitting the job search very hard, maybe sending out one or two resumes a week, but not expecting much. Eventually, I interviewed at a medical center for an Internal Medicine office which I'd be working under a doctor.

I got the job and left the Shell job abruptly saying to the manager at Shell that I was offered some big research job out of town, and that I'd took it, so I could no longer work at Shell gas. That wasn't the truth, but I felt I had to increase the factor of my job worth by tenfold to make me seem like an important person on this plant. This job was different from the family practice job instead of doing the back office (rooming patients) I would be answering the phones doing the front office work.

Things at my new job seemed well. My starting hourly wage was ten dollars and fifty cents an hour. That pay rate was fine with me. I enjoyed my new job at first. I worked steady Monday through Friday 8 am to 5 pm. I was still drinking during the beginning of my job and within a few months, it increased. I originally was drinking a few beers a night starting at 6:30 pm, but within those months I quickly increased my drinking to a full twelve pack of beer. At that time, my choice of poison was Milwaukee's Best. I was drinking away my pain and sorrow, but I managed to still seek out new friends in St. Louis. My pain still surrounded the death of my friends, Jeremy and Katy. Along with an unsuccessful job search and not friends upon arriving back to St. Louis. The friends I had in St. Louis had turned their backs on me. Being back in St. Louis felt like being in a new town. I had no contact with old friends, so I sought out new ones. During this time, a friend's website came out called MySpace. It was a site that I could build a profile of my likes and dislikes and such. The site also allowed me (people) to browse other people within their own zip code and within a certain number of miles and such or a variety of the two.

While browsing this site and still drinking I found many female friends. Those relationships would be called one night stands, but some of those would last a week or so, maybe a month. When those relationships came to an end I'd push them away before they could push me away and abandon me. It was a self-defense mechanism so I would not be able to be hurt again. I saw it as why allow new people to get close to me if I feared sooner or later they would leave me. This stems back from the solid year of losing people that were close to me while I was in high school. This is another criteria of the Borderline Personality. That would be not allowing people to leave them or having that fear of abandonment. I was on MySpace for a couple of years. I filled a physical need there, and that is what it was no more, just sex.

I was in a pointless sea of pussy, and nothing else. Anytime when one of the women I met would ask for something more I would end our relationship abruptly. It's like I sought out these women to escape the pain of my own reality. That was only a temporary fix, and before I knew it I was back into my deep dark depressive state surrounded by an immense sea of black waves.

I hear stories about most people's twenties being awesome while filled with fun and excitement having relationships that turn into long-term ones and possible marriage. They take trips around the United

States having much fun creating memories that will last a lifetime. This was not how my twenties went.

My twenties were filled with loneliness and dark despair. I often found myself hopeless and saw a painful life ahead of me. I was cutting myself off and on a monthly basis over many issues I was dealing with such as, loneliness, having no real money, no friends, no relationships that were meaningful, and so forth. I believe I was correct, and during this time alcohol formed its grips on me so tight that I was unable to break free from it for about ten years. During the years of my twenties, I had about four major suicide attempts. One landing me in the cardiac ICE. Life had become unbearable and completely dark for my future outlook as the sky is black on a moonless night.

Drugs & Alcohol
Part II

Chapter 9: The Dark Years

Alcohol had begun to form its grips on me at the start of my twenties. It wasn't long before the grip was unbreakable, and it felt like all was lost. Once I arrived back in St. Louis before I knew it my life was falling apart bit by bit while being engulfed in melancholy. My drinking was my only way to self-medicate, and it was all I knew when how to deal with my pain. I had never been taught another way as I saw from my alcoholic father who drank through my entire childhood. I saw him do that and figured that alcohol was the only way to cope, so I used it to self-medicate me.

After leaving the Army my drinking was decreased to a few twenty-four-ounce cans a night, but that quickly jumped up to a full twelve pack of Milwaukee's Best. I choose that beer because it was cheap. There was a period I was drinking two to three bottles of wine a night instead of the beer. I figured the wine would make me more of a distinguished person and drinker, but I was just hiding my alcoholism at that point. I wore a mask of having it all together, but that was a false face. I jumped back to the beer after a couple of months as the wine left me with a pounding headache in the mornings. I believe my beer hangovers stopped quickly after I left the Army. It didn't matter how much I drank I was always able to wake up bright eyed and bushy tailed the next day for work in the doctor's office.

During my first job search after the military, my drinking was used to deal with the shock of how the civilian world thought of me, how I could not be hired with my current skill levels in this field without a degree from a university. At one point for three months, I worked in a family practice office. I began my daily drinking of beer than wine. During this time, I was in constant touch with a fellow medic from the Army. We called him Mo, short for Maurice, and he lived in Alabama, so our conversations were mainly on the phone, and then through text as that had just started to become popular. One day I sent him a message just to check in and see how things were going. Out of all the medics that left our unit around the same time, he seemed to be doing the best as far as job status and pay. After a day or two, I realized that Mo had not replied to my message. I began to text him more trying to get a reply since now it was a week and no message. After a few weeks, a get a phone call with the worst possible news. Maurice's mother called me after the funeral since she had started to go through his phone looking for people he was talking to in order to see if he had said anything to anybody. First, she explained to me what happened.

She told me Maurice had been in good spirits all week and was asked to watch his young niece one evening. No one to this day really knows what happened, but Maurice was watching his niece, and during that time he left the room she was in. Then he picked up a handgun and put it to his head. Then he pulled the trigger, dying instantly while having his brains splattered against the near wall.

I expressed my sorrows to his mother and gave her my condolences. I told her that Mo had said nothing to me. I felt that from our talks that he was doing very well in his life. It goes to show you as I have learned that people can hide their demons very well even from the ones that are closest to us.

Once Mo died I thought to myself there goes another good man who is survived by his family. Moreover, to me, it was another Army buddy gone too soon, and no one knows why except him. It was like a curse that was constantly held over me and people leaving me and dying first. I wondered when will it be my time.

By the time I was working in the Internal Medicine office I was drinking a twelve pack a night, but I overplayed my social calendar to my co-workers to hide my lack of a social life. I was drinking and trying to dull my pain and sorrow. I drank alone in solitude. Then another terrible tragedy comes to my world.

My fellow medic Andrew calls me one day to inform me that our brother Brandon one night, and there was some issue with Tim's wife and kicking all the guests out of their apartment. As the men are leaving the apartment while walking on the dark pavement of the parking lot to their cars. The next thing Tim comes out of his apartment holding a pistol. He proceeds to take aim at Brandon and fires multiple shots at him. Brandon was hit about seven to eight times. He died shortly thereafter. I'm shocked with utter disbelieve. I don't know what to say. Andrew and I exchange words with a promise to contact one another if we become in dire needs. During this time, I begin to think it's my high school death curse all over again. I wondered who will be next? I buried myself in booze to keep a normal face to the outside world, hiding my pain once again, like I always did. I was raised to not show pain by my father, it was a form of weakness he told me. I expressed my pain when my friends in high school died, but when I refused to suppress their deaths and move on, I was ridiculed for it. Hiding my pain is what I learned to do over time.

I never figured out why people can go to awake and the funeral one day and by the end of the reception, they feel the need to go out to lunch. I guess everybody copes different, but me I coped with booze and isolation. It is the way I knew and I wouldn't bother others with my troubles. I was all alone.

During this same time, I was on MySpace seeking out women to sleep with, so I could fill my physical needs. There were even times when my desire to spend time with other people lost out to my drinking thus I had to cancel my plans with them in order to drink alone suppressing my pain. It got to a point where I was just looking for women to come to drink with me at home, and then sleep with me, thus filling that physical need I so desired. It came to a point when the women I slept with were just added to a list allowing me to feel that I was over-achieving in the relationship category of my life, but that was just a false reality. One can't have a relationship with someone they don't even know.

One night I was talking to a lady on MySpace and impulsively decided to meet up with her that same night we were emailing each other. We drank at one of her favorite bars, and we had met a friend of hers there too. After drinking for several hours at the bar we headed back to the house of another friend of hers. Keep in mind I had been drinking since about 4 pm alone. Then at the bar around 7:30 pm till 10 pm. I drove to her friend's house and drank there until about 2 am. Most people wouldn't have dared to drive after the first drinking session at 4 pm, but not me I was a professional drinker. The short of the long of it was at 2 am I choose to drive home. Not the best idea I've ever had. I was a good forty minutes from my home, and I almost made it home until I fell asleep at an intersection about 8 minutes from my house.

The cops were kind enough to wake me up and take to me jail. I was charged with a DUI. My consequences were a weekend in a hotel to attend alcohol classes, and after that, I would attend weekly AA meetings while having to get a form signed to prove I had been there. This was officially my second DUI.

In my alcoholic mind having two DUIs by the time I was 22 years old was no big deal. My thoughts quickly dismissed them as not a big deal with my continued choice of drinking. My first DUI was on the night I got engaged and, I barely had anything to drink, about three 40 ounce beers. I could completely drive with that amount in me. I was a soldier and we drank. The second thing, I had been drinking all day and night, but I was almost home. I just needed a quick nap at an intersection, no big deal, right? I hired a lawyer to see to my second DUI got lowered to a less severe consequences, but the judge was shocked when she asked me if I had anything to say, and my response was I was just taking a quick nap before I arrived home. The only thing I really got out of my second DUI was it was safer to stay at home and drink, which I did most of the time. Drinking alone was my safety blanket. There were times after that when I did drink and drive. Who really cared about my safety anyway, not me.

I'm now in AA once a week for an entire year. I had no desire to learn anything there as the same for the weekend classes at the hotel. I even drank while I stayed at the hotel. So, in AA, all I cared about is having them sign a piece of paper. I asked them to sign it before the meeting so I could just take off, but they wouldn't. Then I expressed my views on drinking and explained to them that I would still drink. I even told them I was going to drink after every meeting, but finally, they got the point. Then they started to sign a whole month's worth of signatures. As I'm sober now I often wonder if I did any damage to those people who were trying to get sober. If they were on the fence did my jarring words bring them back to drinking? I guess that is why they started signing my forms before the meeting and letting me leave.

Then I would not have to come back for signatures for a whole month. Time went by, and I was done with my year of AA. So, I moved on still with my heavy drinking. It was one of my only vices at that time.

I had turned twenty-three and was still working at the internal medicine office. I had become quite chatty with a pharmacy tech that my office called frequently and vice versa. Her name was Tiffany. She was one year younger than me. I figured since we were both young that she was most likely on MySpace too. I looked her up and sent her a message on there. At this time, we had never seen each other, and with the MySpace message, we could see each other pictures. I sent the message over the weekend, and she called me Monday morning to ask if that was me. I said, "Yes." We made plans after that to meet up and hang out. She must have thought that I was cute after seeing my pictures in order for her wanting to meet me. I thought she was absolutely gorgeous. She was another goddess just like Kelly, my high school girlfriend.

Tiffany and I hung out a few times and fucked a few times too. I believe it was after three times when I realized that this girl was something special, and I asked her to be my girlfriend. She said, "Yes." Then we fucked again that night. Our dating life was going well, we spent a lot of time at our favorite pub drinking a few pints. I drank more then she did, but since I had a high tolerance by now it would go unnoticed by her.

Thanksgiving had come and gone, but I spent that Thanksgiving with her and her family. When I met her father, I made an inappropriate comment about how good her tongue ring felt, oops. He wasn't too happy about that. Adult drinks were scarce at her family's house, but I am glad I had a flask with me to nip off of to make it through the evening. During this point in my life, I was unable to even skip a night without drinking as I would face withdrawing symptoms, such as the shakes in my hands and the sweats at times. After dinner, that night Tiffany, her sister, and I went to see the movie, "Just Friends" with

Ryan Reynolds. For some reason, we saw that movie twice over the course of our relationship. Up next was her mother's second wedding.

I attended Tiffany's mom's second wedding one because there was an open bar, and two for the reason I wanted to spend the evening with Tiffany. I really enjoyed my time with her and even had thoughts of someday asking her hand in marriage which came about on the night of her mom's wedding. The evening was fun, plus that fact that I was drinking whiskey sours all night, not to mention I started drinking beer at my place a few hours beforehand. At the end of the night, her mom asked me if I was good to drive home when I played down my drinking to only a few whiskey sours as I told her I had been sipping them during the event taking forever to finish one, which was not true. I'm a professional liar too, people seemed to always believe what I told them. She had no clue that I had drunk about ten beers before the event. During the dinner, I sat at the head table at Tiffany's request. Her mom had the whole reception filmed while being at the head table I was in the video, but Tiffany and I broke up shortly after this event. All I can do is think about how when her mom views her wedding video on later dates she'll see some random ex-boyfriend dude sitting at the head table.

Tiffany's and my breakup was hard on me. My mood was dark, black, with a huge void in it as I lost the one girl I would want to marry. My drinking increased greatly after we broke up. A lot of my actions were very impulsive after the breakup. For example, it was Friday afternoon about a week after the break up from Tiffany. Around lunchtime, I got the idea of getting a tattoo in a symbolic form of our relationship and its break-up. All of my tattoos have some sort of symbolic meaning behind them. Once I got back from lunch I tried to get out of work early when I got back, but my boss wouldn't let me go for the reason I gave her of getting a tattoo. She did let me slide out about fifteen minutes early though since I was such a good worker. It was also a payday, so I didn't have to worry about not having enough money.

I leave my work and hit up the ATM, and then I'm on my way to the tattoo shop. It is the only shop I get tattooed at. Once I arrived I find out my artist is not working, but I don't care. I tell the shop people it doesn't matter who tattoos me today. The tattoo lady goes in the back to see who is up for doing the tattoo, which I watch her lengthy tattoo covered legs walk down the short hallway. I look around and noticed that the tattoo shop was quite full and that all of these people were here before me. That meant I could be waiting a very long time into the night for this tattoo. I would have waited till the end of time for this tattoo on this particular day, due to my mental status, and the chaos going on inside my head.

A tattoo artist walks up and points his tattooed covered finger at me, so I go over to the tattoo guy. I explained to him that I wanted an old looking TV set with the "Rabbit Ears" on top of the set. In addition, a heart on the television screen that is cracked down the middle. The meaning behind the TV is that Tiffany's last initial starts with, "V", so the television covers her initial. "TV." The broken heart would cover our relationship and break up. The idea behind this idea is that I have the tattoo, but I don't put her specific name on me, or her initials. That might have been too crazy, even for my own madness. It was placed on my right outer ankle as far away from my heart as possible.

The artist tells me to wait one while he goes in the back to draw it up. Before I know it, he is back. We begin to walk over behind the counter where the tattooing began. I went ahead of everybody that was in the shop before me, but I feel that was because of my relationship with my tattoo artist, and the rest of the shop as they knew me well. The artist is done before I know it, and I head home, but I stop to get some beer. I proceed to get drunk texting Tiffany impulsively with random statements of desperation. Then I send her a picture of my new tattoo. She responds that I'm completely nuts, which I may have been, but in my moments of madness things seemed so clear. After that my darkening of self-was seen all around me as a tornado surrounds a house before it picks it up, and throws it back down.

My black mood was noticed at work. We were about to get a medical assistant to come over to my office to do the back-office work as I did the front office stuff. She would be coming from a GI office, but as she was aware of my break up with Tiffany she stated that she didn't want to come over if I was not fun to be around due to my black moods. I caught up with her and told her I was okay and dealing with the breakup much better now, so she agreed to come over, her name was Chrissy. Without knowing it then she would become a very close friend and confidant of mine.

The funny thing is that after Chrissy had come over, and when a few weeks had passed she began to console me about my breakup, which ended up being a major help to my psyche. But I was still drinking daily because that would never stop. Chrissy was aware of my drinking, and how much I truly drank. She never harped on me about it, she just accepted my drinking never pressing the issue that I might be an alcoholic or judging me. I feel this was one of the things that allowed our friendship to grow into what it did. She was the first person in a long time to accept me for me. It was the beginning of a beautiful relationship.

After my breakup, I decided to move out of my mother's house and into an apartment in Shrewsbury. I was less than a half a mile from work, so my travel was short, which is great when your running late or have a hangover, or just slept past your alarm. My new apartment was great, it was a one bedroom, 650 square feet, and had big large rooms with a breakfast bar. This is a spot where I can drink alone while killing my own loneliness or just to fill the empty hole in my inner self. That is what I did, drink. Over the five years, I lived there the few friends I had left managed to drag me out every once in a while.

My ex-co-worker Britney convinced me to go to a lesbian bar. It was around 7 pm when she called, and I had already been drinking since 10 am. I passed out around 1 pm and awoke again at 4 pm, and then I started drinking since I had nothing better to do. I drank to escape my own physical body and mind, because I couldn't even stand my own company, especially on that night. I went out with her instead that night, some company is better than no company all the time. Humans desire to be around one another, and that it is a healthy desire.

We went to Novak's (a lesbian bar). The reason for going was Britney's friend's sister got a big promotion at work and wanted to celebrate. She was the lesbian hints why we went there. Her boyish looking girlfriend was there too along with a few other people. I named the boyish girlfriend Justin Bieber. So, Bieber is talking about how much she can drink and such. I laugh at this statement, and she challenged me to a drinking contest. I gladly accept. I get the hot waitresses attention and order a slew of shots and two different types of beer times two. The girlfriend is shocked at the first round, but I only tell her we have just begun. I asked her, "What can't you handle it?" So, before the contest started the girlfriend had about three beers already and was stating it for the record. Britney knows I'm an alcoholic and asked me how much I've already drunk today. I reply in a whisper with a sly smile that I've been drinking since 10 am, plus a short nap. That amounted to a case of beer and about half a bottle of Jack.

The drinks arrive on two trays like flying saucers coming from outer space. I explained to her that we have to finish within minutes of each other. Then we will order more drinks. I do all the shots back to back and begin chugging my first beer. As I was finishing that tasty beer when she was taking her third shot, but when she slammed that tiny glass down; she threw up all over the floor. I laughed because I was ready to go three or four rounds of trays, but oh well. I won, and that night I fucked Britney. We were on again off again fuck buddies. Which to me was just another physical connection that I barely connected to?

Eventually, I got over Tiffany, but after that, I grew closer to Chrissy as she helped me get through that break-up. She also was there to listen to me about my other relationships and my troubles. It worked both ways. We knew each other's intimate secrets from sexual ones to everyday life. We were each other's confidants and friends; I felt she was more than just another co-worker to me. After I have had known her for about four years; she had many trials and tribulations going on in that fifth year. I was aware of all, but one. Chrissy was in the middle of a divorce and struggling. She initiated the divorce, but no one is immune to the trials and tribulations of life. She was taking Vicodin for her pain. She did not obtain a prescription legally though. As she was calling out prescriptions from our office in other people's names, then picking them up herself. She wanted to hide her occult pain from her outside world. Then one day the other shoe dropped so to speak. It was devastating to me, and I wished I'd talked to her about it before it got out of hand. I felt it was all my fault. Just like my other friends, I managed not to be there for them in their time of need, but I was in an alcohol clouded mind and things fell by the wayside.

It was a cold Tuesday morning. I get a call from Wal-Mart saying a person was here to pick up a prescription, but the tech knew the name and person, and Chrissy didn't match that name and person. He explained to me that she couldn't provide identification and left. My doctor was off on Tuesdays, so I told him to leave a message for my office manager. At that time, I didn't think it was Chrissy, but I was aware she had called out ones before in her ex-husband's name. There was an incident where Walgreens called and told her that the prescription couldn't be processed. Tuesday came and went, before I knew it I was drinking at home alone like I always did with my nights, in solitude and pain. That is what I did with my time, drink and drink alone killing my own loneliness. I didn't know any other way to cope with life, nor was I taught how to either.

Wednesday morning arrives, and I'm at work going about my normal duties. I noticed that Chrissy seems to just be smiling, and not that talkative. Later on, that morning I take the short walk to my office manager's desk and ask her if she got the voicemail from Wal-Mart, Chrissy hears this. Then I proceed to go by my work area and tell Chrissy that I will stroll down to the lab to give a patient his MRI instructions, and appointment time. I'm still oblivious to what is going on in Chrissy mind that day. As I'm walking out of the lab and past the registration desk where Justine informs me that Chrissy just flew out of here like a gust of wind saying something about how her daughter had broken her arm and had to go. This was not the case. I regret this moment for many years to come, if only I was a handful of seconds sooner I could have done something about it or talk Chrissy down.

What comes next over the rest of Wednesday and Thursday devastates me completely. Chrissy doesn't come to work on Thursday, nor does she call in. Chrissy is missing. A wave of concern comes over me when I see that she is not at work on that Thursday. I begin to regret not being able to stop her before she walked out, as I missed her by mere seconds. I felt I would have been able to talk her down from her panic as

I knew her inside and out. I truly cared for her as my dear friend and confidant. Right after lunchtime on Thursday, my work is informed that Chrissy's body has been found in a rental car on the side of the highway heading southwest. They say she took an overdose of sleeping pills and died. Chrissy had committed suicide, but no one knows the true reason why she did what she did, except me. I feel crushed as I let her down in a tragic time of need. My boss sends me home to grieve verses staying at work, but I'm not to return till the following Tuesday. I leave and immediately go to the liquor store to buy beer and whiskey. I drown my sadness and sorrow away through the rest of the weekend with booze. I barely managed to navigate my apartment being drunk and falling into stuff as I go for more booze in the kitchen. There were times when I was just laying on the floor pawing for the cold beer cans in the refrigerator.

I'm informed the wake will be on Sunday in the early evening around five or six pm. I drink beer early Sunday morning believing that I could pass out and wake up somewhat sober to face the crowd of people at the wake. It's now 4 pm, and the clock is ticking away. I still haven't passed out yet. I ran out of beer, so I begin on the whiskey. I'm sitting on my black couch staring blankly at the TV as shows and movies played, but I am not in-tuned to them. The time has come.

I am drunk, but I tell myself that I will go to the funeral house anyway. I'm driving on the road that is mildly wet as the day has been a drizzly rainy cloudy day. I pull down the hill that leads into the parking lot, but I can't bear to go in. I find myself sitting in a parking spot as I see my fellow co-worker's car pull in. I just can't bare it. I pull out and head home, but I stop at the gas station to buy more beer. My plans are to just get as drunk as I can, then I will attend the funeral on Monday morning.

On the morning of Chrissy's funeral, I meet my doctor and our office manager in our medical building. A lot of the women at work had to be a work but could leave for the funeral only, but I was off work completely as the normal rules don't apply to me in Chrissy's death. At this point in the morning, I am stone cold drunk, but no one would ever know as in the latter part of the night I switched to vodka to kill the smell and continue killing my grief.

We leave the medical building, and head to the church where Chrissy's services will be held. As I take my seat in the pew I feel uncomfortable in my seat, because by that point in my life I was an admitted Atheist. I felt being in a church was like a sin to atheism. I looked around to see Chrissy's many friends and family that showed up. I think to myself when I die no one would be in attendance at my funeral. I was sitting on the left side towards the back in a light colored wooden pew. The odd thing is that I ended up dating a lady that was two rows up from me, but I'll get back to that later.

All of a sudden, I catch something out of the corner of my eye. It was Chrissy in her light grey casket. They wheeled it up to the front. This whole time I am thinking wow this is really happening, and I still don't believe it. I felt I never got true closure with

Chrissy due to the fact that I couldn't bring myself to go into the wake and see her one last time. After the church session had concluded we followed the funeral procession to the graveyard. Chrissy was buried, and kind words were said about her. I'm deeply saddened, and I felt once again lost in life.

In weeks that followed I was drinking more and more while isolating myself from the rest of the world, and any friends I might have had left. They wore worthless anyway in my view. My behavior was reckless and impulsive. I drank until I passed out only to awaken to myself laying in a pool of blood, piss, and vomit. I realized where the blood had come from as I looked down upon my arm to see an elongated wound crusted over in dark dry blood. The vomit was mainly liquid due to me not eating much during these times; it was pretty much straight alcohol that came up with stomach acid. When I realized my pants were wet all I could think of is not again. This scenario had happened many times in the last few years before I got sober. My true dark times had no spot of light to offer hope.

In my latter twenties, I no longer used MySpace to find women, but I did find a dating site that pretty much was a site for people to hook up, despite the women's claims of looking for someone to enter a long-term relationship with. While I had a Facebook account I didn't really care for it, because by this time I no longer wanted to hear from old friends. I spent most of my time not accepting them on there anyway. I thought you didn't bother to reach out in my early twenties, so why now just because there is a site to locate friends you've once abandoned them a long time ago such as, a father walking out on his family on a warm Sunday afternoon stating he is going for cigarettes, but never comes back.

A few weeks after Chrissy's passing I find a random woman on the dating website. We make plans and had our first date. It was on Good Friday, and her name was Jennifer. It was a nice sunny April day and all of the employees finished work at noon. Since Jennifer and I both finished work we decided we would meet at a pub around 12:30 for drinks. I arrived there first and ordered a drink, it was a Bud Light. I figured that I shouldn't hit the hard stuff so early on our first date. She arrived and looked stunningly hot. We begin chit-chatting away while the drinks kept coming as water falls from a waterfall. During this time, I take notice of a lot of people sitting in this pub drinking on an early Friday afternoon. I concluded that these people were a bunch of alcoholics or something odd was happening. I shared this information with Jennifer who explained to me that it was Good Friday, and a lot of people got off early on this day. Then again if they were alcoholics I was sitting right there with them, in my place among them. Here I felt I fit in at, among other alcoholics. The date ends in the early evening as the sun is setting, but the warmth of it still hangs out for a bit longer. We kiss in the parking lot and go our separate ways. The next date comes about the following Friday, and we decided to have drinks at my apartment.

Jennifer is late coming over, but by the time she arrived, I was already drunk as I had been drinking since I got off from work at 5 pm. As she came through the door I knew she wouldn't know I was drunk as my tolerance for alcohol has risen to the level of Mount Rainer's peek. I am a professional drinker by now. We begin drinking and chatting away while we wait for her friend to come over, and have some drinks with us. During this event, I'm having a good time, and am heavily intoxicated by this point in the evening. I explain to Jennifer that I have been pretty bummed out since my close co-worker had passed. I did mention Chrissy's death on our first date, but not her actual name. She asked me what was my co-worker's name, and I replied Chrissy. Then she stated her last name. I was shocked to hear her say it. It turned out that we both knew her, and had attended her funeral. That is where I then found out that she was sitting two rows in front of me. Small world isn't it? Out of all the people in this big wide world and all the gin joints I meet someone that we were both connected to, but just in different mediums.

Jennifer and I dated for a handful of weeks before our relationship ended. We spent our time fucking, drinking, and smoking weed. After a few weeks, I wanted to put a label on our relationships as boyfriend and girlfriend, but she didn't want to. That was how our relationship fizzled to an end, but not without me asking one of her friends out to piss her off, but that was another one that got away, Jennifer that is, not the friend. That makes the running toll of two, Tiffany and Jennifer. Those women were women I saw myself growing old with, but it was not in the cosmos for me. That was how I accepted the breakups.

After Jennifer, my daily drinking continued immediately after work, and first thing in the morning, plus all day on the weekend. My job was stressful as we didn't have Chrissy there so a lot of work fell on me when I already had a full workload. We had temps, but they were never really useful. Around this time, I started to become shameful of my drinking, but I choose to hide it once again.

Normally I bought my beer at the Shell gas station in Crestwood, but they began to recognize me knowing exactly what I wanted to buy. So, I would rotate gas stations and stores such as the beer I bought was rotated between three gas stations, two Shell's (Crestwood) & (Webster) and Quick Trip (Shrewsbury). Sometimes I went to 7 Eleven in Webster too. I always bought my liquor at Schnuck's, but since that was such a big store I never felt they knew me there. Some of my favorite boozes were whiskey, scotch, vodka, and rum. I pretty much covered a wide range of liquors. The reason I would rotate stores was that I felt if the same people saw me purchase alcohol day in and day out that they would have figured out that I was an alcoholic, thus the shame I felt.

To sum it up work was way too stressful, my drinking was out of control along with my cutting. I dated many women where the relationships were a one-night stand or a week-long stand. It is difficult when I was having sex with these women, and a wound opened up and began to bleed on them. That kind of kills the mood, plus it can be a little hard to explain to someone who barely knows you. There were times when I was drunk and alone where I began to cut my brachial artery. I figure that it is an easy artery to reach, and I could bleed out quickly as that artery was close to the heart and much bigger than my radial artery. I've nicked my brachial artery twice in my life. I laid there allowing blood to spurt out of me as someone pushing in the plunger on a syringe; I laid there as the blood pulled on the floor by my bedroom that was black and purple themed. I never bothered to clean up any of these stains. When women would come over they thought that there had been a murder there, and my apartment was a crime scene. One would think that this is a mood killer for sex, but I dated some whorish women who weren't bothered by the blood stains all over my apartment. On a side note when I moved out of my apartment I got all of my deposit back and then some, go figure right? The place was completely trashed.

Things are not well in my world at this point in my life. I'm swimming in a pointless sea of pussy, drunk all the time, and work sucks. One day my doctor calls me into his office at the end of the day. He has begun to tell me he was leaving the practice at the medical center, and he would go into practice for himself. When I hear this, I think oh great I just lost my job, because I knew there would be no other spot for me to go to at Southwest Medical Center. As he was finishing his speech I just turned and walked away. He called me back to say that he was asking me to go with him and that I would get a dollar fifty more an hour. I said yes, but I really didn't care. My life was on a hell-bound train that was one way with no return ticket. A few months go by, and we move into his new practice which was about two miles down the road.

The office opened the day after new year's. Things were going somewhat well as everybody working there got settled into their job responsibilities and what not. After a month or so people began to slack on their work, and that worked got pushed off on me, which is on top of all the work I accepted when I agreed to work in my new doctor's office. This lead to much stress in my life hints why I drank at the end of the day to numb myself. The pain was too much to bare anymore. Inside my mind was completely chaotic, which caused me much inner turmoil. My office manager pushed the additional work on me because she knew I could get it done due to my efficient work ethic. All this did was increase my drinking daily. I felt alone in this world; all I did was work and drink. There wasn't much room for anything else besides a rise in my anxiety. That brought much additional noise inside my head, and I heard voices at times.

Even with the thought of driving an extra two miles to work caused my anxiety for me to rise like whiskey fills a shot-glass, fast. I live my whole life planned to a strict schedule such as, when I drink, leave for work, get gas, wake up, pass out, even the spots I parked in had to be the same spots. Any deviation from my schedule caused much anxiety. I would become panic-stricken, with an increase in my breathing almost to the point of passing out or hyperventilating. It is hard to describe the actual feeling, but when my anxiety hits me I feel the world closing in on me. Sometime I would have a strong urge to flee from wherever I was at. Eventually, I was able to work my new drive to my job into my schedule, and that reduced my anxiety a little.

My doctor had hired another military man to work in the back office as his job was to room and screen the patients. He was another fellow medic like me so we had an instant bond of brotherhood and understanding. What a lot of people don't know was he had helped my alcoholism graduate to a new level. He had a friend who brewed his own moonshine, and this brew was beyond putting a number proof on it like over 180 proof.

He would bring me one or two containers at work that came in clear mason jars. Some of the booze came in a clear liquid and others were brown in color. Those had a cinnamon taste to them because the brewer dissolved cinnamon sticks in

294

them. They tasted great, and both of them went down like water for me.

One day I came home on an early Saturday afternoon, and I pulled out the brown mason jar thinking it was tea as I needed something to quince my thirst. I began to jug it, and before I realized what I was jugging I had finished half of it. Most people would call that a day for drinking, but not me. I started drinking the beer in my fridge shortly after that while drowning myself of the pain I was in, and zoning out to some random dramatic movies. I'd prefer movies that had a troubling and disturbing type, which allowed me to transfer my self into that world instead of mine. Thus, allowing me to feel someone else's pain. I left my pain to take on new fictional pain, but it did relieve my pain just a little.

I began to fall in love with the cinema around the time I joined the Army, but after that, I accumulated a huge number of DVDs. I would rather watch someone's fucked up life in a dramatic thriller then live my own life. During this period, I managed to collect a few things of importance to me.

I started collecting things during my drunken haze of a life. One was Zippos, which started in 2007 and now in the present I have over thirty of them. I collected movie memorabilia such as Harley Quinn's bat, and the joker's mask he wore in the bank robbery and many more. In addition, to my collection of vintage t-shirts. I also collected a huge library of DVDs totaling over 1,000 along with my personal library of books that consists of science, conspiracy, memoirs, biographies, psychology, sociology, occult, crime, cosmos, and encyclopedias, which total over 300 books, and I've read them all. Furthermore, I collected expensive watches that included brands: Bulova, Seiko, Citizen, Rolex, and Daniel Steiger. My conclusion as to why I had a desire to possess these items was because by owning them and having control over them I felt a control over my life as it was completely out of control. I needed something to control. Even though I never would admit that to anybody that showed concern about my behaviors. These items allow a tiny bit of peace within my inner self. The constant drinking covered the rest as I drank in a sea so big it numbed me from my real life I didn't want to be in anyhow.

It has been about a year or more since my doctor's office opened down the road from the old practice. Things are stressful and I'm at my wit's end, but I have no clue what to do, except drink. I arrive at work one morning, and I haven't been there for more than 10 minutes. My doctor quickly noticed that my hands are shaky. He pointed it out to me and everybody looked. I quickly played it off as I had too much coffee that morning. They believed me. The weekend comes, and I test a theory. I told myself that I wouldn't drink Saturday morning to see if I notice the shakes. True enough they come early in the morning. I skip doing my Saturday laundry and go right into drinking some whiskey to stop the shakes.

To help curb the shakes during the work week I start drinking whiskey mixed in with my coffee. On a usual day before work, I would put about one to two shots of whiskey in a few cups of coffee. This works, and I can get through the morning. Then the shakes started coming back around 2:30 or 3 pm. Since I work in my own office I started bringing vodka to my job, so I can nip in the afternoon to make it till 5 pm. Having my own office helped with this greatly as I could close my door, and I wouldn't be bothered. Furthermore, I could often display a mood swing which would allow me to close my door so I wouldn't be bothered. The staff that I supervised often respected that, and they wouldn't knock on my door unless it was urgent on something they needed help with.

  This was my life drinking daily all day and all night. It really got to the point where I didn't want to drink, but I kept on just to fight off the shakes and numb my pain and sorrow. It was very troubling to me to wake up in the morning and not even make it through my morning coffee before my hands would start to shake. To combat the shakes, I would constantly throw my hands down and shake them out to bring them back to normal. That was only a temporary fix; the only real solution would be to start drinking again. A couple of shots in the morning, one during lunch, and a few nips of vodka to make it till 5 pm when I got off of work. Then I could begin to do the real drinking. I'm drinking to combat my shakes, kill my pain, and loneliness. Why would someone need to drink this much? I drank to forget the memories of my past so I would not feel any more pain. I was consumed in darkness, and my wounds weren't made to heal. Someone once said, "It's okay to look back at the past; just don't stare too long." I lived every day in my past, and I was stuck there permanently. Then something finally happened.

 I woke up one day tired of waking up in my own blood and vomit. I was tired of the many identities I held, being too confused on who I was. I decided to get professional help once again in my life, but this time it was my choice. I truly wanted it. I call this part of my life the pre-treatment.

I started with my health insurance plan to see what psychologists I could see. Then I called around to a few doctor's offices where I was professionally close to in order to get their recommendation on some names of psychologists to see. Next, I checked to see if they were in my insurance plan until I came upon the name Dr. Bemer. I called her office and set up my first appointment.

My appointment was towards the end of the workday, but I still had to leave work early to make my appointment. When I arrived at her office building I walked the three floors to her office. I prefer to take the stairs as I am afraid of elevators. We met and began our session with the normal history, family history, and what was currently going on with me.

I explained to her that I hated my life, drank passed excess, was a "cutter", and wished to no longer exist in this horrid life of mine. She expressed her concerns, but I was still closely guarded as I did not trust many people. Some may have called it paranoia. Eventually, she called me on it and told me that if I can't share what my problems are that I am just wasting my money, and she couldn't help me. I agreed and began to open up more with each time I saw her. After many appointments, she had a good suggestion.

It was to get me back in college to pursue something I truly wanted to do. This came from my unhappiness at work and lack of importance on what I was doing. Dr. Bemer helped me with the process of enrolling in college and finding out what my degree plan would be. I was enrolled as a full-time student with a degree pursuit in Nursing and Psychology. This meant I would leave my full-time job in the doctor's office. That meant I would lose my insurance and not be able to see Dr. Bemer as it would be too costly on student loans alone. Before my last appointment, we agreed that I could see her on an as-needed basis.

I started college on a warm summer day, excited for the road ahead that I would face. By the end of the first week, I couldn't form words to speak. This is called pressured speech that I had experienced. My mother thought that I had had a stroke in that first week and she encouraged me to make an appointment with Dr. Bemer.

I saw Dr. Bemer a few days after I called to set up the appointment as I explained it was an emergency. She talked me through my speech problem, and how to slow down my racing thoughts so I could express what I was trying to say. This worked, and my speech soon returned to normal. College still had its hurdles to overcome.

Once I got started on my class-work I found it easy to make A's, and I still started drinking by mid-day, so that is what I did. School work and drink, my pain was still there looming like a tall building that has been abandoned, surrounded in darkness. I could ignore it all I wanted, but it was still there, and it needed to be attacked with alcohol. One day my English paper grade was posted, and I received a B. I truly lost it. I continued with my classes that day as scheduled only to rush home, and I started drinking some whiskey. Furthermore, as I got more drunk I began to cut myself to watch myself bleed. I felt numb and dead on the inside, so I had the desire to cut and see the red sea of blood flow out of me to know that I still had a life-force pulsating through me. Moreover, the next idea I had was to email my English professor.

In my email, to her, I explained how my grade did not match the information I presented in my paper. She agreed to meet with me to discuss it in person in her office. Luckily enough my drunken email did not come off like one normally would have. We talked, and she agreed to allow me to make corrections and re-submit my paper. I did that, and my grade was changed to an A.

College was great I made all A's my first semester, and the second-semester grades were looking to be the same. I was invited to join an honor society called, "Phi Theta Kappa." I was pleased with my first year of college, but I was still drinking while fighting my dark demons. At the end of the year, my GPA was around a 3.8 to 3.9. That was due to my breakdown and taking a few zeros on some of my finals for my classes as I couldn't be around for them. My grades were high enough that it barely affected my GPA.

My breakdown shattered my world as I knew it. The darkness came upon me like a blanket falling upon a person engulfing them completely. The time for complete commitment to treatment and the abstinence from alcohol was needed in order to save my life. I was shipped off to Lexington, Kentucky, where I would spend the next fourteen months or so in treatment.

Chapter 10: The Treatment Years

Before I went off for treatment my world had come to a tragic end. I tried getting sober by myself, in addition, by attending AA meetings. I made it to one month and received my one-month coin. I was proud on that day, but by the time I hit ninety days things weren't the same. On my ninetieth day of sobriety I was supposed to attend my regular Wednesday afternoon meeting and receive my ninety-day coin. It was Tuesday, and I was looking forward to it, but then everything just changed in my mind. A US soldier once said, "When the best tool you have is a hammer, then every problem starts to look like a nail." Since I was prone to suicide, and I had eight attempts already. My problem started looking like a nail once again. I impulsively took off from my home and went to Quick Trip. It was Wednesday afternoon and sunny. I saw the big red and white letters of QT as I pulled into the parking lot past those gas pumps. I bought some whiskey and beer. I arrived home and began drinking, I realized that things would come to an end by tomorrow afternoon. My life seemed glib and pointless. There was a storm forming in my mind, and it was dark in nature.

While drinking those green Heineken beers as the buzz started to come on I logged onto my laptop and began to write my final suicide note. I stated my reasons in my note and explained that it was no one's fault, but my own due to how fucked up my life had become by my own poor choices. I knew I would be dead by Thursday afternoon. I noticed that I was short on beer to drink before I did the deed tomorrow. I was too drunk to drive to get more beer that day, so I called QT and asked them what time they could sell beer in the morning. It was 6 am or something. I drank the whiskey until I passed out on Wednesday early on in the daytime. Once I awoke on Thursday, and then I ran out to buy more beer, while mailing my second suicide note to a friend, Dana. This friend would be the friend to say those few simple sentences to me to get me to realize how alcohol had ruined my life before I entered treatment. Apparently, the guy at QT I called Wednesday evening was still there come Thursday morning, and he asked me if it was me that called yesterday. I told him, yes, but my thoughts were this guy has no clue that I would be dead within hours. It's a strange mystery knowing something like that, knowing the cashier has no clue of what is going on in my mind at that time. Once I arrived home I began drinking beer and whiskey together.

While drinking I began to put together my suicide supplies. Those supplies were six months' worth of several medications, beer, whiskey, a handful of razor-blades, and lastly a rope to hang myself with. The plan was to drink and take the pills. Then I would slit my wrists the, "right way," while hanging myself from a homemade noose. Robert Frost said, "Freedom lies in being BOLD." This was the only way I could grasp my true freedom by being BOLD. Even if it meant my life would end. The pain and misery had become too much. I was stuck in a vortex of darkness that seemed impossible to get out of.

I figured mixing the booze with the pills could take care of shutting down my organs. Then I would bleed out from my wrists while being strangled from the noose. I had it all taken care of. I covered the organs, blood flow, and breathing; it was a full proof way to die. There were only a few problems with my plan. By noon I was completely hammered, and I had just started to take the pills. On a side note, as I took handfuls and handfuls of pills my body knew what I was doing. It rejected some of them and my body regurgitated them. That didn't stop me, I took more and more pills. Then I drank more and more. By the time I was ready to take the final two steps (slitting my wrists and hanging myself). When I stood up on a wooden chair I had become overwhelmed with dizziness. It was hard to maintain my balance. Furthermore, I never realized how hard it was to get my head through a noose hanging from a basement ceiling. It was high up to keep my feet off of the ground when I dropped, but it would have been easier if I had a higher chair. I fell off of the chair a few times before I had given up. I was laying on that cold grey cement floor with my head spinning, and my body felt truly numb for once. I couldn't move, but I finally had reached the state of numbness I always sought after. Melody Beattie once said, "We have lived with the abnormal so long it's become normal. Our hearts have gone Numb." That was my normal, living the abnormal life of pain and sorrow. "Choices in life are easy; it is living with them that is the hardest part." Jeremy Irons once said that in the movie, "The Words." I had made many bad choices in life: not going with Jeremy, not being there for Mo, not being a better friend to Katy, missing Chrissy by a matter of seconds, not being in Washington to watch Brandon's back, and many more, but it got to the point when you add up all my choices and having to live with them were just too much at this point in my life. Eventually, I was found, and an ambulance was called.

The red siren blaring ambulance took me to St. Mary's hospital at full speed. Everything after that was a blur, but in the next day or so I woke up in the cardiac ICU. I was confused and deeply saddened that I was still alive. The nursing staff congratulated me on living, but all I wanted to do was die. I'd failed once again in my life. I had someone there with me to watch me twenty-four hours a day to make sure I didn't do anything, but that person never bothered to talk to me. I didn't care for that too much. I didn't feel right on this spinning planet people called Earth. Jacoby from Papa Roach sang, "The hardest ones to love are the ones that need it the most." I lived through many trials and tribulations, but I felt I was never loved! Not even by my parents. Even though I wanted to be loved very badly. I felt alone in this big wide universe, and I was surrounded by darkness.

After a few days, I was transferred to a VA hospital. From there I would be shipped off to Lexington, Kentucky for long-term treatment. This was the spot when Dana had to help me realized what alcohol had done to me and my life.

Dana had visited me and while I was still denying my alcoholism. She said to me, "Take a look back and see where alcohol was in my past. Then review that look and see where alcohol was surrounded around my problems." That is all she said. I didn't respond at first, but I did think about those words for a few days. They sunk in like people's feet in quicksand. Here was where I realized alcohol engulfed my whole life and caused me many trials and tribulations. Some I could deal with, and others I could not without the help of alcohol. I needed help. Lexington here I come.

When I arrived at Lexington I was on minimal medication, and I was not defiantly stable on my first round of meds either. I arrived on a warm sunny day in July. I remember the day clearly because it was the seventeenth. That was the day Katy was killed by a truck. Also upon my arrival, I started writing in a journal to help me through the upcoming treatment I would face. Since that day I have continued to keep a journal while numbering each one. At the time of this writing, I'm on journal number ten.

Treatment didn't go well at first. I was committed and ready, but that was not enough. I was very symptomatic during the first six months of treatment. Moreover, I was not stabilized on the right combination of medications either. It took six months or so just to get me on the right combo of meds, but those meds would be changed around once again after treatment ended.

One of my diagnosis is BPD (borderline personality disorder). In many books, it says that borderlines are some of the most difficult patients to work with, and my behaviors during the first half of my treatment showed that that holds true, especially when I was as symptomatic as I was. I was highly symptomatic during that time. Some of the consulars even thought that I was not committed to treatment like I was. I wanted the treatment but the chaos in my mind caused me much turmoil. It was like the view of a daycare where all the kids were running around like kids who have ADHD and are off their medications. It was chaos, and I was having trouble with my inner world, and the world outside of my person. Life was difficult, and I thought treatment would be easy, but once again I was having problems adjusting. I believe I knew everything, and I was smarter than all my consulars. I dictated to them how my treatment should go, which is not how they saw it. This caused problems for both of us.

I had opportunities to make friends during treatment, which I did. I had a small handful of friends, but I was around these people day in and day out, but I still kept them at an arms distance. When someone withdraws from contact with others that is often a sign that something is wrong. People generally want contact with others, which is a sign of being healthy. Basically, I kept the other people at arm's length due to the fact that I lacked trust in others. There were a few friends I did confide in at times.

Some of those people were Bret who worked on Wall Street, Shannon, Will, Tim, Adam, and Mic. There were about sixty or so people in my treatment group, and we all lived together. We had rooms that varied from four to eight people per each room. Even with the friends, I had made in treatment I didn't open up to them for about six months. When Shannon graduated and was going back home to Alabama I was deeply saddened. It felt like another piece of me was torn from my soul. Shannon and I still stay in contact with one another, but that is only every few months or so to check in, with each other, and see what's new in our lives.

The people in treatment with me each had one personal consular, and we met with them once a week to check in. During that time, we discussed any personal issues since I was so symptomatic during my first couple of phases I was assigned a second consular, whose name was Mrs. Samantha. I met with them together sometimes, and other times I met with them separate. I felt having both of them helped me greatly during my time in treatment, and turmoil.

During the week we met through the duration of the morning in groups. There were three separate groups we attended. The afternoons were ours to work on assignments given to us and to meet with our consular. There were three phases that we had to graduate through. Phase one was yellow, two was blue, three was orange, and graduation was purple, which is my favorite color by the way. Hints my bedroom being back and purpled theme. We were identified by which phase we were in by wearing the colored bands to match the phase we were in.

Each phase focused on certain aspects of our thought processes. The treatment was based on CBT, which stands for Cognitive Behavioral Therapy. We also learned many coping skills such as, anger management, self-soothing techniques, and handling life's difficulties. Since I had major anger issues or mood swings and had frequent outbursts I took two additional anger classes on my own during my time on the weekends. I feel today those classes had helped me greatly. I went through phase one just fine, but since I was very symptomatic during my first six months by the end of phase two I was told I had to repeat it. This caused me much anger, frustration, and disappointment. I have a condition of LFT, which stands for low frustration tolerance. That means my tolerance for handling frustration is very low, which could include anything from anger outburst, cutting, and dealing with everyday life stressors. When that short line is crossed my outbursts come in a torrid from anything from a sharp tongue-lashing to a whirlwind of anger that could be in a temper tantrum or throwing objects, and yelling at people. I even managed to work on some techniques that calmed my anxiety from my OCD traits. My consular helped me on my checking routines such as, after leaving my locker and not going back to check on it fifteen times. I would say to myself, "That the lock has been locked, and there is no need to go back and check it. It is locked, and you know it is." This helped me a lot with my rituals. Then there was the "cutting" to work on.

I cut a lot during my mid to late teens and all throughout my twenties. The only period my "cutting" was heavily decreased was while I was in the Army. I probably only cut about two to three times while I was in the Army for the three and a half years I was enlisted. Since I was very symptomatic during the first half of my treatment in Kentucky, I cut often. I did it in secret, mainly cutting my inner ankles, and on my outer left thigh above my knee. I did burn myself at the very beginning of treatment with an iron. That injury was on my right lower inner forearm. It was a big triangle from the top third of the iron, and they didn't buy that I accidentally brushed my arm against it reaching for the spray bottle of water on the ironing board. Needless to say, after that I was not allowed to use the iron without supervision. Someone might ask how did I get razors to cut myself. Well, we were allowed to have the onetime use razors to shave with, but they came in packs of ten. They did not monitor how many we bought or kept with us. I broke many of them open to get the blade out to cut, and then I would flush them down the toilet after my "cutting" ritual only to break a new one open days later to cut myself and watch the life-force flow out of me knowing I was not dead inside. My "cutting" ritual generally followed the same routine. I got a blade, a towel to catch the falling blood, and a rag to dress the wound with it in order to stop the bleeding once I had watched enough blood flow out of me. Eventually, as I progressed in treatment I learned coping tools to handle my "cutting."

This one aspect of my many problems was a difficult and big monster to overcome. I would like to say that once I've learned these tools that I never cut again, but this is not a fairytale ending. The skills I learned allowed me to decrease my "cutting," while keeping episodes few and far between. There were times after I got back to Farmington and St. Louis where my compulsion to "cut" won over, but that number is now far less than what would have been before without having these new

skills. The biggest tool I use to combat my "cutting" would be the distraction or delay method. That would be as if I felt like cutting now so then I would put it off by telling myself that I'll do it when I get home, or after a certain TV show, or time at night. By the time it would come to cut generally I would not feel the urge to "cut" at that point. During my time in-between waiting for the cutting event, and the present I would distract myself with other thoughts such as, walking my dog, Mr. Houdini, watching a film, or just thinking about what I had coming up in the next few days, while still living it one day at a time. Believe it or not, but it truly works. For myself, cutting is a way to manage my emotions that are too painful for my words to express. A poem by C. Blount stated,
"How will you know I'm hurting.
If you cannot see my pain?
To wear it on my body.
Tells what words cannot explain."
 This is very true.
        In my last six months, I was stable on my meds, which had been changed

several times. I felt it was the right combination at that time that kept me stable. My medications allowed me to cope with the stressors I was dealing with in a reasonable manner. I was able to slow my anger, racing thoughts, LFT to the point where I could talk out my problems in a reasonable rational manner, and control my cutting with the tools I was given. By the fourteenth month, I was ready to graduate and head home to St. Louis. Before I could come home to St. Louis to live I would stay in Farmington, MO for a handful of months in a half-way house that way I would not experience the world at full force. This is where I met my consular Maria.

I had graduated and was back in Missouri, living in Farmington. Obviously, I no longer had my consular from Kentucky. In my past, I have had adjustment problems when my situation had changed, and this was another one. I'm in the half-way house. I still need to continue my individual counseling which would be done through a company called, "A Horizon of Hope."

There I went through a handful of consulars before I was assigned to Maria.

When I moved back to Missouri my anxiety levels had increased, and I felt the half-way house freedom took my focus away from my work in treatment. A lot of my symptoms had come back. I played mind games with my first two therapists until it got to the point where they shit canned me, and I was moved to someone else by the last one who was the owner of the company finally had it with my games, and she had passed me onto her daughter, Maria. Maria took a different approach with me, and that seemed to work. My trust in Maria was forming with each of our appointments. We were able to talk, and I felt she truly listened to me, in which I could respond accordingly with my thoughts and feelings versus hiding them like I was used to. This allowed me to build trust in her. That is something I don't do easily. She even worked on trying to get my razor-blade count down a little bit since I was a "cutter", and had so many of them at my fingertips. I can say she succeeded in lowering the number of blades I had, but there are still a few floating around my room. What I feel is neat is that I rarely even noticed them around my room these days. I would call this an improvement, and it had been months since I cut myself. We would meet once a week for the time I was in Farmington. After a handful of months, I moved back home to St. Louis. At that time, I met with her twice a month for two hours each time. I was committed to treatment and committed to making the drive to Farmington to continue to meet with her.

During this time, I saw a psychiatrist at the VA too, and she managed my medications. They were changed a couple of times since seeing the VA psychiatrist. She added this, upped that, and stopped this and what not. I was not completely happy with this psychiatrist. I felt I was the one who dictated what meds were changed to what and so forth. Eventually, I fired her, and I was assigned a new psychiatrist. I'll get to her a little later in the next chapter.

A lot of people think treatment has an end date, but that is not true. Treatment goes on forever, but after a certain point, treatment falls into the maintenance phase. Here things may seem easier to cope with one's symptoms as long as I continued working and putting into practice my coping skills. This phase can go smoothly, but sometimes it will hit its rough patches that make life seem unbearable. The point is to work the tools in your toolbox and reach out to your support network when it is needed. The time is to use something other than the hammer as a tool to cope.

At this point, my treatment has ended. Now I am in the maintenance phase. I still see Maria, and my new VA psychiatrist to manage my medications. It is up to me to handle my life's stressors on a daily basis. Furthermore, I'm attending AA meetings to deal with my alcoholism. Currently, I am on the fifth step of its twelve-step program. The next chapter will be my life in the present.

Chapter 11: My Diagnosis

Before I went to Kentucky I had a brief stop in Springfield, Missouri. Here I would spend about a month or so speaking with a psychologist who would eventually diagnose me with BPD, borderline personality disorder. We meet a couple of times a week and discuss many issues and problems I faced throughout my life.

Eventually, on a cold day, Dr. Lindsey called me into her office, I was particularly fond of Dr. Lindsey. She explained to me that I was diagnosed with borderline personality disorder. I disagreed with her as the words came out of her mouth. I explained to her that I had a great personality and could get people to dance to my tune any time of the day.

Dr. Lindsey explained that that is not what it meant, so she gave me a book to read since I liked to read so much. The book was called, "I Hate You, Don't Leave Me." This book was the book that was the "Borderline" book at the time to explain this disorder. This was on a Friday afternoon. I took the book and read the entire book over the weekend.

When Monday arrived I showed up at her office and told her this book explains me to a T, but I still don't think that I have this borderline business. She laughed. She explained the treatment options for me and told me what I could expect with this diagnosis.

Having a personality disorder hit me like a ton of bricks. At the time I felt I was given the answer to what was truly wrong with me. It was a turning point in my life. I could use my diagnosis as a cop out and blame everything on it or I could embrace my condition and thrive off of my disorder.

I choose to embrace my condition and learn everything about it as possible. I read many books about BPD because that was the only way I could come to terms with my personality disorder. I had to understand it to apply it to myself and that way I could learn about my disorder, thus allowing me to know myself more.

I learned this disorder was called the wastebasket disorder because it basically borderline three major other conditions. Those would be Bipolar, DID, and Schizophrenia. A person who would meet only a few of the criteria for each of the above. That meant that they didn't qualify for one of the diagnoses, so the people who come up with the disorders decided since it bordered on all three, it was named Borderline as a new diagnosis. The wastebasket thing comes from the idea that it didn't meet enough criteria so it was a wastebasket to the three diagnoses mentioned above to from Borderline Personality Disorder. My diagnoses.

Once I learned this I thought to myself that I have the answer to what is

wrong with me, but I was still at a loss.
What did this mean to me? Like before I
choose to embrace this diagnosis! I found
out despite this disorder has been around for
decades and it is still not well understood.
Not mention that people are not aware of
this disorder, which means when people are
unknown to something they are afraid of it.
I learned that with cutting.
One of my goals in life is to spread the word
about borderline personality disorder. So
people can understand what this disorder is
and not be afraid of it. When you share with
someone that you have a mental disorder
they tend to take a step back from you,
which is what I am fighting against.

Chapter 12: The Present Time in Years

So far, I have told you what it was like before, what happened, and now I will tell you what it is like in my current present existence. I've been to hell and back on my road to life, and I have the vouchers to prove it. I'm currently an active member of Alcoholics Anonymous. I'm in therapy once a month for two hours, plus I see a psychiatrist to manage the medications that I am on. I don't always promote the use of medications, but if they are needed to help manage severe symptoms than I'm all for it. I'm currently taking a handful of meds that consists of a cocktail of Lithium, Buspar, Gabapentin, Prozac, Trazadone, and Latuda. While these meds are not a cure-all they do help me to manage my symptoms while being able to cope with my reality of life.

I currently attend three to four AA and DDA meetings a week. The DDA meeting is a dual diagnosis meeting, during this particular meeting I'm allowed to discuss my mental health issues along with my alcoholism. I feel this is a meeting of great help to me as I can discuss both issues verses at an AA meeting I would mainly talk about my alcohol issues. I've got around five years of sobriety at the time of this writing.

I work a twelve-step program of recovery. I just finished my fifth step, which is the step where I shared my fearless and personal moral inventory with another human being. That step was a huge step for me to complete since I sat on it for about two years. I finally shared it with Maria my therapist who I see in Farmington. I felt there was enough trust between us to share my inventory with her. Now I am at the start of my sixth step of AA and looking forward to it. Currently, I read, "Daily Reflections," which is an AA book where I read a page out of it each day. At the end of the year, I would have read the complete book as each page is dated for the days' date. I don't use a God figure for my higher power, but I have one.

I created my higher power in my image since I am an atheist, but this higher power was not the one that would make me rich, successful, or find the one I would come to love on my demand. This higher power would guide me along my path of sobriety, while I would be able to turn to it in times of need. I have trust in my higher power that it would put what I need in my life when it was needed. By believing in my higher power and trusting in it I feel that I have a guide standing alongside me in my walk of life.

Even with my higher power by my side, I do get lonely most times as I have not found a partner in life to share my feelings, emotions, and thoughts with. This is a battle that I have been dealing with for almost five years now. It feels like I walk alone down this lonely road on a boulevard of broken dreams. My fight is not over though. It's me and my higher power, and I trust in it to put a special person in my life when the time is right or anything else it thinks I'm fit for, now that I am sober.

My daily life consists of working four days a week or so. I work part-time for a catering company, so my shifts mainly are on the weekends during the night, but I do work someday shifts too. At the time of this writing, I would have been with the catering company for two years. I feel at this time I make good money, but not enough to pay rent. Since I've started with the company I've taken on many new responsibilities such as, server, food runner, shop work (which is done at the warehouse), ESU (which stands for early set up), that means I go to event spaces in the morning or early afternoon to set up all the tables and place settings for the upcoming dinner, lastly, I do the ceremony chair set up for the weddings. The last job has given me the responsibility of having my own key and contractor ID badge for the gardens, where the weddings are held. My new step after the new year is to ask them if they will train me as a bartender, this hasn't happened, because I never asked. I feared they would say, "No." And that could have left bad blood, so I didn't ask.

Some of the readers may be thinking is it the best thing for me to do being an alcoholic. While I work around alcohol as a server, pouring wine and getting drinks for the people at my tables I feel that I would be fine working the job as a bartender. I've discussed this topic with my therapist, and we feel I would do fine working that job since I haven't had any, urges to drink doing my job as a server. Furthermore, I have the correct coping skills to handle any urges that may come about. In addition, to my working a strong program of recovery is the key for me to stay sober. Being around a lot of alcohol at the weddings has never gotten o me. When I pass the wine actually the smell bothers me. I can truthfully say the alcohol goes unnoticed by me at events.

I don't have much of a social circle as I find it hard to make new friends when

I'm thirty-six. At this age, it is not like grade school where I can go up to someone and say, "Hey, do you want to be my friend?" Not to mention the fact I'm guarded around most new to newish people I meet due to my trust issues, but I'm working on it by being open to new relationships. Deep down inside I long for friendship because Earth can be a very lonely place without anybody special in my life. I'm still fighting the good fight on this issue though, and I'm open to making new friends. I even started hanging out with a co-worker, Nancy.

 About a year ago I bought a 2011 BMW 328i, and she is the love of my life. The payments are very reasonable. I spend my spare time improving her and washing her while doing a full detail each time I wash her. I call her Lucy after the movie, "Lucy" with Scarlette Johansson. So far, I have honestly put about $1,550 into improving my car, cosmetically. I still have plans for another $500 dollars' worth of improvements for my car too. My movie collection is still growing.

Either during the mid-day or at the end of my day I still lose myself in a film. I normally watch films before work or once I arrive home. I generally purchase about ten DVDs a month or so. I've come to the conclusion that I use this form of escape as a coping mechanism to deal with my life. While I watch movies, I can become the characters from the movie while taking on their personal feelings and thoughts verses dealing with my own. This is not the best coping skill to use, but it's still a distraction from my own self and my world. It's always nice to be able to take a break from yourself once and a while. My personal library will always be growing.

I purchase my books at a discounted bookstore. I read about 2 or 3 books a month, but my queue of books to read it about 4-5 deep. Reading is another great escape for me, even if they are nonfiction books. The books I read quince my thirst for knowledge, even being thirty-six my quest for knowledge will never stop. I've re-enrolled in college at Maryville University.

I've completed at the time of this writing one and one-half years of college. I'll be starting my sophomore year in the past spring. I have listed a double major in psychology and sociology. In four years I will have obtained my bachelors in psychology and a masters in sociology. My goal is to work in research while I pursue my Ph.D. in neuropsychology. I'm looking forward to attending classes at the university while hoping they will be challenging. Furthermore, while I began classes at Maryville University I will be open to making new friends since I lack many in that department. Moreover, making new friends that are academically inclined as me seems exciting with just the thought of it. I feel it will be nice to find friends that hold their academic life in importance. So, to bring up cutting one more time.

As I said before that I would like to say it's a fairy tale ending, but my coping skills when it comes to "cutting" make the episodes few and far between. There are scars on my heart that will never heal but with time they decrease in size. But I have still had to revert to cutting at times. I have even cut myself during the writing of this book, but when I do the deed it has fairly decreased in how often I cut. I just do my best to stick to my coping skills in my toolbox. This one particular thing I do is hard to explain in words at times, and most people just don't understand why someone would harm them-self in such a way. My distraction plan of delaying a "cutting" episode is putting it off till a later time, reading a book, watching a movie, walking my dog Mr. Houdini, or seeing the positive in my life helps me greatly.

This concludes my daily life as to what it is like now for me in the present. I have a different outlook on my life now. I try to see things in the positive verses in the darkness of the abyss. I feel better about myself as a whole, and I'm often content with my life as it is allowing me to take things one day at a time. While doing that I'm able to be more relaxed throughout my day and allow my stressors to roll off my shoulders dealing with them in normal rational ways. Now my abnormal is

changing, and I'm living in the normal. I
can deal with things in a rational way, which
allows my life to be lived in the light.

Chapter 13: The Tattooed Years

My body is tattooed like a graveyard, filled with the most important people I have ever encountered in my life. Each of my tattoos has some sort of important meaning to me and only me. That's why they are there. I will take some time to go through all the tattoos I have. Plus, ones I plan to get.

My first tattoo was of the number 10 as that was my hockey number and I was married to that number. What that means is that I wouldn't skate for a team unless number ten was available. Yes, I was that much of a Pre-Madonna when it came to my number, hints why I got that number tattooed on my body. Its location is on my right forearm.

The next tattoo I received was a symbol I designed for "St. Louis" as I didn't want to be like all the other people with the Cardinals logo tattooed on them. I got this to remind me of where I come from, St. Louis that is. Not to mention the curse that came along with it, which is the curse of never being able to truly get out of this horrid town. It was truly a town of pain for me.

I did a self-tattoo which was my graffiti name of "Spun." As that is how I felt where my life was going. I was constantly spinning in circles trying to figure out how to get out of the dark side of the abyss. I did the tattoo with a safety-pin needle and India ink. This tattoo took a long time as I had to puncture my skin individually to get the ink to set in. I used one-inch lettering for the tattoo.

The third tattoo I received was of my middle name, "Jules" on my upper left arm. This tattoo comes from the heart for me as I was named after Jules Vern the author who wrote back in a time of candlelight, but he wrote about what they would call science fiction. He wrote about spaceships going to the moon, nuclear-powered submarines and so forth. I had read all of Jule's book by a young age and appreciate his works. Today I am very fond of the name Jules and the people would know his full name Jules Verne and his books.

The next tattoo comes while I was in the military and in AIT for my medical schooling. I had made the choice to get tribal around the name Jules on my arm. That stems from my grandmother being bohemian with family history from that. Let the Indian strive through me.

Then came the Jesus on my upper right arm. Despite being an atheist, I felt it was still due because of my friend Jeremy and how he never doubted God, but I did later on in life. This was the start of a decade-long tattoo that I would have placed on me throughout the years.

 I continued Jeremy's tattoo up with a cross that bared his name and that was of a cracked marble cross to represent his life, his pain, and tormented soul.

While reminding me of his memory. He was a special person in my life. A month or so after that tattoo I gotten my niece's name tattooed on my left chest that said, "Breanna, My Heart." The writing was tatted within a cloud on my chest. The idea of this tattoo was that I would never have kids, given my bad boy image. She would be the keeper to my heart, whatever she wanted I would give her.

The following tattoo would be off the lettering of Jeremy's tat, which read, "In Memory of and had the dates August 6th of 1981 with John 8:36 to Sept 1st, of 1998 R.I.P. I know what you may be thinking that how come an Atheist will get a bible verse tattooed on him. It is more than just that. My friend Jeremy was a special person and at the time of his death, he believed deeply in God, despite committing suicide. I honor him on my arm. Literally, I gave up an arm for him!

When I got back to St. Louis I got the word, "Love" tattooed on my inner left forearm with a city behind Love as love was stacked two by two as LO over VE with the "O" being tilted in honor of love park in Philly, which is a park where a lot of skateboarders skated at.

The tattoo that followed that was a bands symbol. The symbol is called the HIM space pope dude. It was in honor of a band called HIM and I got that tattoo to honor the band and my faith towards them. They are from Finland.

During my goth years, I was given the blessing of having a tattooed heart on my left wrist. The black heart represented me and how I expressed myself. Which is through my left arm since I'm left-handed. So my dark words are expelled through my dark arm and out through my left hand. As I wrote dark poetry and spoken word. It's an expression of how I write.

Then after that tattoo, I showed up at my artist's shop. This time I want an old timepiece clock like the timepieces people carried in their pocket. This I get but I want the glass screen cracked as it has been bashed in. The key of the tattoo was the time it would tell. That would be at three o'clock. The three stands close to me. As the three months, I was married. The three years I did in the military. Plus a few more set of threes. So, I got the tattoo.

The next tattoo was grim. It was about the girl named Tiffany that I wanted to marry. But that wasn't in the cards. I got the "TV" on my right lower ankle to keep those initials as far as they could be on my body. But the bunny ears were there too. And that is that to my break up tattoo. The screen had a broken heart on it to symbolize my pain of this relationship that had ended.

Sometime down the line, I found out about a social movement that was for suicide awareness and since I had a high number of suicide attempts. I thought I would look into it. People were getting a ";" (semi-colon) tattooed on them. The idea was don't end your life with a period and put a semi-colon instead of a period, that being where your life would end and write the next sentence instead of ending your life.

I get the semi-colon on my left outer lower side of my abdomen. I jumped on board for suicide awareness. Given my history with suicide. The semi-colon is black and purple (my favorite colors).

The tattoo that followed it up was a black crow on my right front shoulder. The reason I got the crow tattoo was because of its history and mythology as it carries someone's soul. Plus the raw intelligence of this bird.

A few months passed by and I added a piece to Jeremy's tattoo, which was the grim reaper on my inner upper right bicept. The reaper represents how death stalked Jeremy and took him too soon. But then would go on to stalk me forever with no luck.

All my tattoos are black and grey except for my middle name and my niece's cloud tattoo, along with the semi-colon. I've always been a fan of black and grey tattoos. The only thing I have left to get is the background for Jeremy's tattoo to make it a half sleeve, but what has taken me so long to finish the tattoo is that I would finally have to admit Jeremy was gone, with the completion of his tattoo.

The same goes for Katy's tattoo. Hers will be of three roses with the stems wrapped around each other and a banner with her name saying, "In Loving Memory of Katy Orf." This tattoo will be in color thought as to pay tribute to Katy's beauty. Once I get this tattoo I would have to admit Katy is finally gone, which will be a painful day for me.

Chapter 14: How My Life Turned Out in Years Present

Given everything that has happened to me; my life is quite put together now, and I'd survived the roller coaster of one hell of a life. I managed to survive the life I once lived, given how self-destructive I lived my life and how I abused my body. The cutting has decreased a lot and I only cut "Now" as a last resort, when my life feels like it is in pieces.

Just because I've stumbled and fallen upon my way, doesn't me I'm lost for good. I've fought my way back to the top and gone towards the light. I never thought there would be a light at the end of this tunnel, but now I can see one. It looks bright, as my future does.

This is no fairy tale ending though as I have my good days and bad ones, but the majority of them now are lived in the light and are good days. When I have a dark day, I am able to cope with my problems now in the present. I use numerous coping skills to get me through my turmoil. Some skills I use like I know the back of my hand, others take a little more practice at deploying them, but I try.

Given the place I used to be in; today I can say that I've come out on top and many people were there to help me. The therapist that would not give up on me, the ones that sat with me in crisis and help me work through my problems. I thank them, because without them who knows where I'd have ended up.

My life has been a crazy life once lived, but I've been able to handle and cope with that portion of my life now in the present and I can say I generally live a normal life, given that fact that some people would have never thought I could live a normal life.

I work and go to university where I have a double major in psychology and sociology, where my career looks promising upon graduation. I no longer feel, "Spun" (my graffiti name.) Now the spinning has slowed to the point where I can stop and smell the roses. I feel I have control at the wheel so to speak, and that things are no longer out of control. Someone once told me if you have to take control of something it is usually that thing that is out of control.

One thing I can tell you is that in life there are no dress rehearsals. If you're lucky enough you may get a due-over, but from what I learned you have to live with your past and the choices that you have made. Like the old saying says, "You've made your bed now lie in it."

And Lastly,
"Your experiences make YOU who you ARE, and that's what makes you unique!"
Matthew J. Gewinner

A Word from the Author: Conclusion

Originally, I wrote this book as a catharsis for me to get all the evil out from me. I figured writing my story would allow me to process some of my emotions that I kept bottled up and locked in a safe. I can say writing my book has helped me greatly. While writing my memoirs I found a second reason to share my story.

I hope the readers out there can read my story and empathized with me while being able to see the things that had happened in my life for the good or bad. Furthermore, any reader that has had similar struggles as I had had in my past; that they can find hope in my story, and seek help when it is needed to overcome their personal struggles. Remember one cannot get help until one truly desires it. It is a difficult road to travel down, but it is still possible with hard work.

My advice to the struggling person out there is that things might get worse before they get better, but one should keep at it. With hard work, things do start to improve, and the sun becomes brighter, take it one day at a time not five or ten days. That is how I live my life, one day at a time. It works.

I can truly say I've seen myself grow and improve, while others have told me that they have seen great improvements in me too. From my everyday behaviors to my severe mood swings; things have changed, and I'm grateful for that, but it takes hard work to go down the road less traveled is a hard road to turn around on, but it can happen with the right work. Everything is possible when you see hope on the horizon. It's nice when the sun shines during your day versus living in world of darkness filled with black clouds. Change is difficult, but it's possible. Hope is out there, and I believe that. My future is unknown, but my fate is made by me, and it looks bright.

I encourage anybody out there dealing with dark troubles to see help and not give up. One's life may seem bleak, but if you are ready to make the change then change can happen. I encourage others to speak out and share their story to help others out there. Remember sharing your story helps both you and the people you share it with.

THE END.

I would really appreciate now that you have finished reading my book if you could review my book on Amazon. It would mean the world to me. Thank you in advance. I welcome and want feedback, so I may improve my writing.

Book Club Questions to Consider

1. What could have caused Matthew's childhood violent rage towards his neighbors?
2. Could there have been more done in Matthew's teenage years to get him help?
3. Did Matthew's early head injuries affect his life later? Or was the trauma just minor?
4. Was Matthew pushed too hard when playing hockey that it caused him to lose the love for the sport or was it the right amount to get him into the NHL?
5. What would you have done in Matthew's life to improve his overall living?
6. Were Matthew's mental health symptoms truly masked while in the Army or did they just lay dormant?
7. Do you think if Matthew would have stayed in therapy with the female therapist his life would have turned

out different, instead of joining the Army?

8. How do you think Matthew's tattoos helped him in his recovery when dealing with the loss of his friends?

9. If you can change one event in Matthew's life what would it be?

10. Do you think Matthew ever got over the loss of his friends or did he just learn how to cope with his loss?

Made in the USA
Las Vegas, NV
07 September 2021

29775345R00203